Technology and Competition in the International Telecommunications Industry

For
Nicky & Caroline
Meg
Angela & Hattie
(and Angel in New Orleans)

Technology and Competition in the International Telecommunications Industry

David Charles, Peter Monk and Ed Sciberras

 Pinter Publishers, London, New York

© David Charles, Peter Monk and Ed Sciberras 1989

First published in Great Britain in 1989 by
Pinter Publishers Limited
25 Floral Street, London WC2E 9DS

British Library Cataloguing in Publication Data

A CIP catalogue record for this book is available from the British Library

ISBN 0 86187 9937

Library of Congress Cataloging in Publication Data

CIP Data available from the Library of Congress

Filmset by Mayhew Typesetting, Bristol, England
Printed and bound in Great Britain by
Biddles Ltd, Guildford and King's Lynn

Contents

List of Figures

List of Tables

Foreword

This book on technology and competition in the telecommunications industry could not be more timely, as action to complete the internal market for telecommunications accelerates towards the European Community's 1992 deadline.

Telecommunications is playing an increasingly important role within the economy, as well as within society more generally. Telecommunications technology is changing rapidly – increasingly converging with the computer industry, forming a conglomerate 'IT & T' sector, as well as with broadcasting towards an ITT & B sector. Telecommunications lines are increasingly carrying data as well as voice, with a whole new value added service industry emerging. Both the network and the host terminals are embodying more and more intelligence, requiring large investments but also making possible a far greater range and quality of services – for both industrial and domestic users. As persuasively argued in the text, the subscriber equipment is essential, not just as a sector of growing importance itself, but also for the development and use of the new services.

Hence the European Commission is vigorously pursuing a dual strategy for the telecommunications subscriber equipment industry: ensuring a fully competitive European market, while at the same time securing the conditions for universal access. This is being done within the framework of regulatory change for the entire telecommunication industry, as proposed in the European Commission's 1987 Green Paper and adopted by the Council of Ministers in June 1988.

This book also gives an intriguing analysis of the industrial changes in store for Europe: securing increased flexibility and efficient relative scales of production will pose a challenge for business strategies throughout Europe. The enormous benefits from The Economics of 1992[1] will come largely from just such a process: increasing the market to a size capable of responding to increased competitive pressures on a sound business base, allowing greater economies of scale and scope for large enterprises as well as increased niche opportunities for innovative small and medium scale

---

[1] March 1988 European Economy.

enterprises. The importance of economies of scope is brought out clearly in this study; the increased range (scope) of products and services produced by a single firm gives another twist to the competitive position of such firms, allowing the spreading of overheads, including the huge and growing costs of R & D, over more products.

1992 – the Europe-wide market – is becoming a reality. New technology and new opportunities require change. For its part, the European Commission is determined to follow through the necessary regulatory and industrial changes in order to maintain – and develop – Europe's excellence in the area of communications services and equipment in the world market.

Dr Herbert Ungerer
Commission of the European Communities

Acknowledgements

The research reported in this study was made possible by the support and cooperation of many people.

We would particularly like to acknowledge the help freely given to us by staff at all the participating firms, and by representatives of other organisations. In addition, we have benefited greatly from discussions with colleagues at the Centre for Urban and Regional Development Studies, University of Newcastle-upon-Tyne. We would like to thank them for their contributions to this project, although any errors or omissions remain our responsibility.

This project was sponsored by the Leverhulme Trust, whose generous financial support allowed us to undertake research 'in the field' in six countries.

The logistics of international fieldwork call for the highest quality administrative support. This was provided most ably by Joan Cassell-Hill, Audrey Crow and Nicola Parker. Secretarial support of equally high calibre was provided by Betty Robson, Sue Robson and Denise Weites.

Introduction

Background

The telecommunications subscriber equipment (TSE) industry, apart from being an important and advanced industry in its own right, occupies a nodal position in the technical and commercial development of the 'information technology' sector. It is a nexus for technological and commercial advances in components, electronics and software; TSE products provide the main interface between telecommunications users and networks. Its performance is of considerable importance for the development of major new services in the information economy.

Radical regulatory, commercial and technical changes are sweeping the industry. All leading industrialised countries have been liberalising their telecommunications industry, exposing their national markets for the first time to some degree of international competition. Technical change, in part spurred on by this new pressure, has transformed the products and manufacturing processes of the industry. It has also blurred the traditional distinction between telecommunications and computer technologies in both production and use.

The imminent creation of the Single Market in Europe in 1992 and its implications for firms both in and out of Europe lends particularly relevant focus to the whole issue of structural adjustment in the industry. The major benefits of the Single Market are expected to come, not from the immediate removal of remaining barriers, but from the opportunities to follow as a consequence of the restructuring of industry and markets.

These developments have necessitated major changes within the TSE industry, with many firms seeking to change their scale of operation, their structure and their strategic orientation. Although a large number of companies have already responded and reorganised, the industry remains in a state of flux, and further changes are likely to occur as firms attempt to adapt to an evolving competitive environment.

The opportunities, or need, for mergers or collaborative arrangements internationally between European, North American or Japanese firms as a means of achieving the scale and structural conditions necessary for competitive success, are an important issue – one which this book addresses.

Between 1981 and 1986 a series of studies on technical change and international competitiveness was undertaken (Sciberras & Payne 1985, Dickson & Sciberras 1985). The final study, of the international telecommunications subscriber equipment industry, was concluded in 1986 (Sciberras & Payne, 1986).

The objective of the studies was to understand the relationship between technical change and international competitiveness in industry, and to assist policymakers in industry and government to make appropriate adjustments to the conditions identified as being required to achieve competitive success.

Two broad issues appeared to be the most important determinants of international competitiveness in the TSE industry. These were:

- firm size and structure – including vertical and horizontal integration; and
- the manufacturing process – including new production techniques and the requirements for their successful implementation.

The feasibility of firms adopting appropriate structures and manufacturing and investment strategies is heavily dependent upon adequately large size. The past research found that it was difficult for smaller firms to obtain these advantages although they were often aware of the potential.

Large size and integrated structures alone, however, are not sufficient conditions for competitive success. Firms must be willing and able to develop management perspectives and implement techniques and strategies which allow them to realise these benefits.

The aim of this book is to explore in more detail than was possible in the previous studies, the specific issues which were considered the most important influences upon the successful adoption of technical change by firms, and upon their international competitiveness.

Telecommunications subscriber equipment

The telecommunications equipment industry can be divided into three major sectors according to the role of products within a telecommunications network. These are public switching equipment, transmission equipment and subscriber equipment. A public network is composed of switches linked by transmission equipment and cables. At the terminating point, on the customer's premises, is the subscriber equipment (TSE) also known as customer premises equipment (CPE).

TSE includes two broad categories of products – private switching products and terminals. Private switches interface directly with the public network. In some cases this equipment may appear to the user to be functionally 'transparent', having no discernible barrier between the user's terminal and

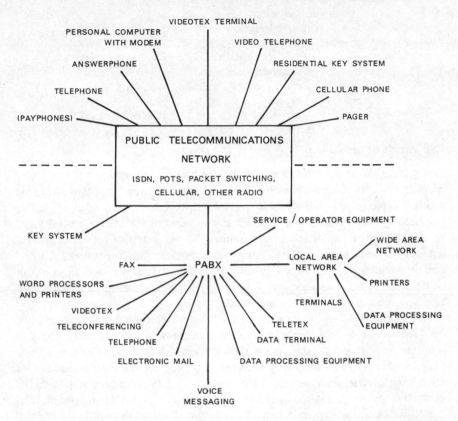

Figure 0.1 Telecommunication subscriber equipment in public and private networks

the public network. A private switch acts as a terminal to the public network, even though it is effectively the hub of a private network. It switches calls from the public network through to internal terminals and also switches calls between two or more internal lines.

Terminals formerly comprised telephones and – within separate networks – telex terminals. These were connected directly to the public network or via a private switch. However, as new networks for data transmission and radio communication have been formed, new types of terminals have appeared. An increasing range of terminal products may now be used with the telephone network, for example facsimile machines, modems. Figure 0.1 shows the range of terminal equipment used within public and private networks.

TSE comprises three main groups of products:

● private switching products – private automatic branch exchanges (PABX)
         – key systems;

- voice terminals – telephones
  - cordless telephones
  - cellular telephones; and
- non-voice terminals – modems
  - data terminals including PCs, teletex, telex
  - facsimile
  - video terminals including videotex
  - pagers
  - integrated voice/data workstations.

TSE switching products

The private automatic branch exchange (PABX) has generally replaced older non-automatic exchanges, and the PABX is assumed to be the basic switching product referred to in this study. A PABX comprises a central switching mechanism with a main switchboard and a number of internal extension lines. In simple terms, it switches telecommunications circuits between internal extensions, and between internal extensions and the public network. Control circuitry within the exchange also allows particular features such as group or conference calls, automatic call-forwarding, call-transferring and authorisation restrictions on types of calls made.

New digital PABXs are capable of switching both digital voice signals and data transmissions and can combine the functions which formerly required two separate networks. Also, using new workstation terminals, data and voice may be switched simultaneously between two people allowing for discussions and simultaneous data display. Non-switched data networks can also be controlled by some PABXs with local area network (LAN) interfaces.

PABXs range in size from very large networks with thousands of internal extensions and hundreds of external lines to small key systems with as few as three internal and one external lines. Larger PABXs are housed within racked cabinets often separate from the control panel. Key systems may be housed within a desk-top box, or, in the case of the very smallest, within the telephone instrument.

Voice terminals

The basic voice terminal is the telephone, essentially an apparatus for converting between sound waves and electrical signals. Currently most telephones are still analogue, in that the electrical signals are analogue rather than digital signals, even though the form and operations of the telephone may have changed considerably in recent years. Local exchanges in most countries still handle analogue signals although trunk relays are increasingly digital. As new digital local exchanges are introduced (particularly ISDN), and within digital PABX networks, new digital telephones are being introduced.

Separate from the change from analogue to digital signalling, the functions and features available on the telephone have grown. The old dial telephone could only receive calls, or dial up calls. Modern push-button telephones can store numbers, redial, dial with the receiver on-hook and use external loudspeakers and microphones. Further features can be added in conjunction with digital or ISDN exchanges. A distinction should be made between features that can be gained using microelectronics within analogue telephones, and features that make particular demands upon digital exchanges, and can only be used with digital signalling.

In addition to such changes in the basic performance of the instrument, new telephone terminals are available with cordless operation, relying on radio transmission between the handset and a base station connected to the network. A second generation of cordless telephones (known as CT2) is being developed which will allow use of a generic base station rather than just the nearest of the same telephone model (for example within the home). The CT2 therefore would be able to use public base stations in a similar way to the true mobile phones, but over a short distance only. Call-charging data would be managed automatically within the network.

The third form of voice terminal is the cellular telephone which is a true radio telephone operating within a separate network of radio 'cells'. This network has interfaces with the public telephone network but may be operated by a separate carrier. Cellular networks are analogue at present, but digital operations are planned, including a pan-European integrated network. Technical problems remain with the design of digital handsets but it is anticipated by firms in the TSE industry that with greater component integration these problems should be resolved within the next four years.

Non-voice terminals

Non-voice terminals include terminals for data transmission in terms of digital signals, digital representation of images, and also paging systems. Although these types of equipment are peripheral to the main focus of the study, which concentrates on PABX and telephones, their significance is growing rapidly. A brief description is provided of the main types.

Modems

These are modulator/demodulator units for converting digital data into analogue signals for transmission over non-digital telecommunication networks. Although currently of great importance they will become obsolete with the installation of ISDN.

Data terminals

Personal computers, computer terminals and specialised teletex terminals are increasingly used on digital PABX networks and, via a modem, public networks.

Video terminals
These would include computer terminals with visual display units, as opposed to printers, capable of receiving and displaying images as well as text. Audio telephone links may be incorporated into the same terminal.

Facsimile machines
These convert images on paper into digital form for transmission over analogue or digital lines. Current 'group III' machines encode images as data which are transmitted in analogue form, but new 'group IV' machines will used ISDN for fast digital transmission, the greater transmission speeds allowing colour coding in addition to monochrome.

Pagers
Simple radio signal receivers – although new models allow short messages to be received. New digital cellular systems will allow an increasing range of facilities such as store and recall of messages, print out, response or one-way voice.

Economic and technical significance of TSE products

Telecommunication networks form part of the necessary infrastructure of modern society. Business and public services are completely dependent upon these networks for control and information flows involving both voice and data. New data services enhance this dependency daily, with even domestic transactions and services becoming increasingly dependent upon telecommunications.

The European Commission has estimated that the employment of over 60 million people in Europe will be dependent upon information services and telecommunications by the end of the century (CEC 1987).

Although this growth in usage has been aided by improvements in the network infrastructure, and will be further enhanced by ISDN, the network can only transport information. New terminals are needed to provide the human interface for these new services, and computer/data access to the network also depends upon specialised terminals.

Another dimension to the changing environment is the location of functions within the network. As additional features become commonly used within networks (call-forwarding, conference calls, short-code dialling for example) the location of the hardware and software responsible for such features has become more flexible. At one extreme such functions could be built into the local network switches, giving a 'centrex' form of operation. In contrast, functionality could be placed within the TSE apparatus. The ramifications for providers of such equipment are considerable, and Postal Telegraph and Telecommunication administration (PTTs) are also involved in these strategic choices. Even within the TSE industry a similar debate occurs over the structure of PABX networks with some firms looking to produce distributed LAN-based systems rather than the traditional star-structure of systems based on telephony.

The regulated market for telecommunications equipment and services contrasts vividly with the open, competitive markets for computing and audio-visual equipment. The convergence of these technologies has created considerable regulatory problems. Whereas once there were clear demarcations between telecommunications, audio-visual broadcasting and audio-visual recording, in the future the same equipment may be useable for all three activities. Cable systems offer the potential to deliver telecommunications as well as television along with interactive data services and access to video libraries.

Methods

The study was concerned with competition between relatively large companies in the major telecommunications markets, recognising the dominance of these firms over the total world market. The major markets of North America, Europe and Japan were seen as the arenas within which competition was developing and therefore all three were included. From a European perspective there was also a need to examine the challenge of potential competition from Japan and North America. Even in small national markets it is increasingly the large global firms that are the 'major players', and these smaller markets are increasingly becoming passive receptors of technological and market trends established in the core economies.

The study therefore sought to investigate the following issues, obtaining quantitative detail where possible.

Firm structure and size

- The volume of production and its influence on the costs and competitiveness of firms in the industry.
- The relationship between competitive advantage and large-scale production.
- The influence of different corporate structures on costs and competitiveness.
- The advantages of diversification and the extent to which potential benefits were being exploited.

The manufacturing function

- The significance of the manufacturing function for competitiveness.
- The implications of adopting new products, production processes and organisational forms.

● The nature of the relationship between new technology, flexibility within manufacturing and competitiveness.

Central to the study was the need to see how all these different elements came together to determine the competitiveness of firms.

In practice the complexity of the issues unearthed – and the very limited value of existing theoretical formulations – made it extremely difficult to obtain other than quite general quantitative information. Measurable constructs of scale and scope were found to be meaningless because of their lack of replicability. In practice, they proved unhelpful in portraying the real-world advantages or disadvantages associated with large size or multi-divisional activities. Many of the advantages attributed simply to 'scale' in conventional economic theory are in fact inseparable from the operation of diversified activities by firms and many advantages attributed to 'scope' require large scale to be realisable in practice.

Variations in the availability and quality of data necessitated a pragmatic approach to research. The firms themselves often did not have quantitative data for these factors. Some firms which had such data felt unable to release it on grounds of commercial confidentiality. Therefore the research is largely based upon qualitative assessments of advantages and disadvantages supported by such quantitative evidence as could be obtained.

Given the logistical problems of interview research in an international industry, it was not possible in this instance to undertake a comprehensive survey of all industry participants. A sampling framework was therefore required to obtain a meaningful view of the sector.

The major firms in the mainstream TSE product industry were identified from the USA, Japan, Germany, France, Sweden and the UK. From each of these countries smaller firms were also selected to establish alternative perspectives on operating within that economic environment (see Table 0.1). This allowed comparison between TSE firms of a wider range of size, and operating under specific national conditions.

Table 0.1 Sample of subscriber equipment manufacturers

Country	No of firms	Size range in TSE (£m approx)
UK	6	20–150
Germany	3	100–1000
France	2	80–2000
Sweden	2	
Japan	4	250–2000
USA	3	40–1000

Contact was established with senior management in the TSE relevant divisions within firms. Interviews were conducted with staff from one or more of several functions – chiefly manufacturing, development, marketing or strategic planning. Executives were very helpful in giving sufficient time to discuss the issues of concern in the study, and in some cases more intensive meetings were possible involving several people over the course of a day.

The advantage of previous research in this area was that background material already obtained enabled the targetting of the research directly onto the issues identified as being of principal importance for the present study, without losing the wider commercial and technical context within which changes were taking place.

Outline of the book

The importance of economies of scale and scope is frequently asserted in industry studies, yet the meaning of these terms is rarely examined in detail. In most instances scale and scope are regarded as vague causal factors in studies of changing market structure. Few attempts have been made to examine the sources of such economies either in theory or in practice. Part I of the book concentrates on the theoretical aspects of the study. The literature on scale and scope economies is presented in Chapter 1 in an attempt to separate out the practical benefits that may be realised by firms from the unattainable ones presented in conventional theory.

Chapter 2 follows with a pragmatic assessment of the literature on the realisation of competitiveness within manufacturing. Manufacturing is the arena within which scale and scope benefits may be expected to occur. It is also subject to pressures of technological and commercial change, especially in product-supply flexibility and lead times for product innovation.

In Part II, evidence from the TSE industry is examined, addressing the questions posed by previous work and by the review of theory. Chapter 3 gives a descriptive account of market trends in the industry, providing the background for understanding the operating environment of the firms.

Chapters 4, 5 and 6 analyse the strategy and observed behaviour of the firms in terms of scale benefits, scope benefits, and their manufacturing operations.

Part III looks forward, with a review of future trends and developments in the TSE industry in Chapter 7. A final section summarises the implications of the findings for the industry and for further research in the telecommunications industry.

Part 1 Theory and Concepts

1 Economies of Scale and Scope

Analysis of scale and scope in the TSE industry

A striking feature of markets for telecommunications and information technology (IT) products is the dominant share held by very large corporations. The size or scale of output (in terms of value or quantity) of producer firms is frequently cited in analyses of international competitiveness as a factor in cost competition and as a barrier to market entry by new producers. Widespread attempts by existing TSE producers to gain additional scale through mergers, joint ventures and other cooperative arrangements suggest that the size of firms is seen as an important determinant of their competitive success. In the TSE sector at least, minimum efficient scales of production – equivalent to national monopolies in some cases – appear to favour the global corporation rather than the small 'high-tech' firm. The size distribution of firms in the TSE sector suggests that economies of scale confer competitive advantages on large producers.

Recent developments in the analysis of industrial competitiveness have emphasised the importance of the scope of activities undertaken by firms (Goldhar and Jelinek, 1983). Diversity of production activities, functions and products is characteristic of large multiproduct firms of the type that dominate the international TSE industry, (Sciberras and Payne, 1986). Analysis of competitiveness in the TSE industry must therefore take account of economies of *scope* as well as economies of scale.

The purpose of this chapter is to identify those aspects of scale and scope economies that are most directly relevant to the competitiveness of firms in the TSE industry. Theoretical treatments of economies of scale and scope are briefly reviewed, as a preface to a consideration of the sources of scale and scope economies in practice.

The types of scale and scope economies discussed here reflect aspects of *real-world* production rather than simply abstract theoretical concepts. In view of the relevance of scale and scope economies to competitive strategy in the TSE industry during the present period of radical structural change, it is important that investigations of multiproduct costs are based on concepts of production relevant to producers in the real world. Similarly, the managerial and strategic aspects of scale and scope economies are treated pragmatically. The limitations of economic theory are put into perspective by reference to issues raised in the management and business literature. This investigation, then, is driven by practical objectives rather than theoretical elegance; to identify the nature and role of economies of scale and scope as determinants of competitive advantage in the TSE industry.

Economies of scale: critique

In neoclassical economic theory, increasing returns to scale are said to occur when the marginal cost of production is less than the average cost of production at a particular level of output. Therefore an increase in scale will lead to a reduction in average unit costs of production so bestowing a cost advantage on the larger plant. This may continue up to a certain optimum scale at which point marginal costs exceed average costs and diseconomies of scale set in. This crude definition is widely accepted (see for example Lipsey, 1971), yet it rests on assumptions and theorising which are open to question.

Starting with the traditional microeconomic theory, the short-run average-cost curve (SRAC curve) describes cost condition as each plant incurs fixed capital costs and variable costs of labour and materials. Therefore, as production increases, unit costs will fall, up to a point at which the plant operates optimally, above which diseconomies set in as the plant is forced to produce more than its designed capacity. Thus if output rate is plotted against unit costs, a U-shaped curve for average costs is defined.

Looking to a range of plant sizes, separate cost curves indicate, for each given size of plant, the optimum level of output for lowest unit costs. The least-cost curve describing these curves is the long-run average-cost curve (LRAC) or 'scale curve'. This describes the costs that could be achieved by a plant changing scale rather than simply the cost conditions at a given scale.

'Specialisation' refers to the increased division of functions within the firm, as larger size allows effective use of dedicated or single-function equipment and personnel in place of non-specific or multifunctional forms. It is generally assumed that specialisation leads to greater efficiency due to design factors in the equipment, lower setting-up requirements and the benefits of

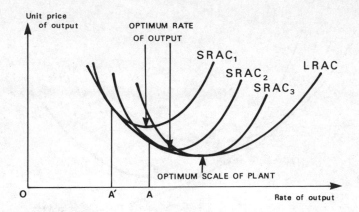

Figure 1.1 Short- and long-run average-cost curves

increased familiarity with an operation. The theory of increasing returns to scale predicts that the scale curve also will take a U-shape, as specialisation due to larger size allows marginal costs to lie below average costs. Again however, a point will be reached at which marginal costs exceed average costs and so average costs will rise and *diseconomies* of scale then hold (Figure 1.1).

As the scale curve is built up from all possible SRAC curves for an infinite range of sizes of plant it therefore forms an envelope curve around these SRAC curves. Several writers assume that the LRAC describes the point at which the SRAC curve is at its optimum level – that the LRAC describes the set of lowest costs achievable by an infinite number of optimumly operated plants (Pratten 1971). However as Bilas (1967) has pointed out, the SRAC curves are not tangent to the LRAC at their lowest point, except for when the LRAC curve is at its lowest point, assuming U-shaped curves (see Figure 1.2).

Thus for a plant operating at its optimum rate of output but less than the optimum scale, there must be larger plant sizes for which costs are lower despite operating at a less than optimum level. This implies that rather than achieve the optimum output for its size, a firm should aim to increase the size of its plant – even though operating sub-optimally to achieve lowest costs.

However, in the real world the implication is clear: given the lag in scale adjustment, a particular plant may seek to operate at its optimum output but find that larger competitors will be achieving lower costs despite sub-optimum levels of output. The only way of achieving competitive parity is therefore to increase the scale of plant.

Gold (1981) points out four assumptions in the theory:

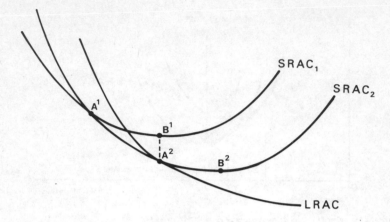

Figure 1.2   Detail of cost curves

1 The short-run average-cost curves showing the capacity utilisation of plants of fixed scale are U-shaped.
2 The minimum-cost points for the long-run function decline up to a point above which they rise again.
3 Plants producing identical products by means of identical inputs and technologies can cover a number of different sizes.
4 The overlapping of adjacent cost curves shows the diseconomies of under utilising large plants compared with fuller utilisation of smaller plants.

Gold argues that these assumptions are weak both theoretically and empirically. In an earlier study, Gold (1968) shows that the U-shape function is increasingly unlikely as static conditions are relaxed. That analysis challenges the benefits of increased scale in capital goods and in investment which underpin the second assumption, and posits a number of other cost elements that increase with scale (for example administrative and support staff, wage levels). The third assumption is shown to be weak in terms of engineering analyses which suggest narrow scale ranges within which these conditions will hold. Gold's empirical evidence shows that in cases of wide disparities in plant scales, there are also substantial heterogeneities with respect to technologies, products and factor proportions.

Given the weakness of these three assumptions, the final point which is dependent upon them can also be regarded with considerable suspicion. Indeed, there is no reason why small plants should be able to provide products with comparable qualitative characteristics for the same markets (Gold, 1968).

The concept of technology in the neoclassical framework gives a clear illustration of the problems of abstraction. In static analysis, the state of technical knowledge is assumed to be given, constant and 'best practice'. However the neoclassical concept of technology subsumes all aspects of the *organisation* of labour and capital for the process of production as well as the *form* of labour and capital employed.

Any single plant or unit of production (A) will require in addition to its productive activities an administrative or decision-making unit to support it. A second plant (B) which comprises a number of such units of production (ie it is a multiple of A), will therefore have constant factor ratios. However the decision-making functions must be different. Even where this role is fulfilled by a single entrepreneur the *organisation* of labour and capital in plants A and B will be different and hence there will be a difference in the technology applied.

In the real world of course it is unlikely that the organisational differences will be limited to decision-making. A plant with several production units (for example multiples of A) will employ other organisational techniques to make use of possible economies of specialisation, such as group purchasing, amalgamation of some production elements, and so on.

This difference between savings arising from reorganisation and savings arising simply from size is very significant. The neoclassical assumption is that the scale curve shows the possibilities for production at an *optimum* use of the given technology – that is there is no x-inefficiency (Silberston, 1972) – thus the curve is based upon a very narrow view of production possibilities.

In practice, an industry may comprise firms with a series of plants of different sizes employing slightly different 'technologies', even if only in organisational terms, to produce similar but not necessarily identical products. This could entail a wide range of possibilities all of which are feasible within a set of real prices in the industry, accepting that as products are not equal and markets not perfectly free, prices vary between products and firms.

One could assume that for each technology employed there might be other hypothetical scales of plant that could, were it possible for them to exist, lie on a strictly defined scale curve. However, because of the technology problem described above, scale curves cannot be drawn; the hypothetical scales of plant simply could not be built with the given state of technology.

In much empirical research (see for example, Pratten, 1971) the technology is ignored as scale is taken to represent the relative size of a plant within a broad category (for example at the three- or four-digit Standard Industry Classification level). Thus in these cases the analysis ignores factor proportion, product difference, product technologies, the form of manufacturing operation, and the degree of processing and/or fabrication of materials (Gold 1981). Clearly, these factors are relevant to analysis of the role of scale economies in any sector. This study attempts to overcome both the unrealities of neoclassical theory and the practical difficulties of making realistic empirical comparisons of plants in the TSE industry.

It is important also that what is meant by scale is understood. As technological change can profoundly affect the nature of 'minimum efficient scale of production', then clearly scale is a dynamic concept. Plants and firms may be measured in terms of size of workforce, output or turnover but all of these will change relative to each other over time. They will also change relative to the market. For example, a plant producing 100,000 units with 1000 employees and a turnover of £20 million may have a 20% market share in its first year. Subsequently unit output may remain constant with a fall in employment, a rise in turnover and a fall in market share. Does this constitute a change in scale and, if so, in which direction?

The important issue for competitiveness however is the size of a particular firm relative to its competitors at any given time. Market shares of firms, for example, can only be judged in the context of size of national market relative to other countries, with due consideration given to international trade and investment.

A further issue concerns the level of analysis. Should analysis of scale economies be at the level of the firm or the plant? Most theoretical and many empirical studies focus on the single *plant* as a comparable operating unit for analysis. However there are also economies of scale to be realised by the multiplant *firm* although these may be of a different form to those of the individual plant.

In the case of plants, scale economies are generally described as 'real economies' derived from changes in the quantities of materials and labour used to produce a unit of output. However at the firm level, other factors become dominant such as pecuniary economies from bargaining power, and specialisation of management and other non-production activities (Bain 1956). Economies of scope and of vertical integration also become more significant at the firm rather than plant level, and these may relate to the scale of production.

To explore the existence of economies of scale arising simply from production scaling up, the plant level will be most appropriate for analysis. However this current study seeks to determine the role of scale in competitiveness within a number of real firms in a real industry. Hence it is necessary to look at the cost of the *firms* as well as plants and to examine scale in conjunction with scope and other issues. None the less, even a comparison of plants would entail problems of determining scale economies of the neoclassical type, due to the level of heterogeneity in technology, and the degree of diversification of production *within* plants.

Economies of scope: critique

There are two types of multiproduct firm. The first type is that which produces a variety of diversified outputs for purely financial reasons – a common rationale for 'holding companies'. The second type of firm is that which produces a range of related products, with the intention of exploiting specific technical or commercial links between them. Such firms are common in the TSE industry, and it is the exploitation of links between different TSE products that allows these firms to realise 'economies of scope'.

According to the originators of the term, 'economies of scope' exist 'where it is less costly to combine two or more product lines in one firm than to produce them separately' (Panzar and Willig, 1981, p. 268).

The cost advantages enjoyed by the multiproduct firm over equivalent single-product firms are made possible by the sharing of one or more inputs between different product lines:

> Whenever the costs of providing services of the shareable input to two or more product lines are subadditive (ie less than the total costs of providing these services for each product line separately), the multi-product cost function exhibits economies of scope. (Panzar and Willig, 1981, p. 268).

Investigating economies of scope in a firm therefore means looking at which inputs (including service inputs) are shared – and how they are shared – between which product lines.

Bailey and Friedlaender (1982) suggest two general sources of scope economies: excess capacity in the utilisation of inputs, and the use of inputs which exhibit some of the characteristics of 'public goods'. The latter case refers to 'quasi-public' inputs, which are required for one product line but which are then available (at little or no extra cost) for use in other production activities within the firm. A third general source of scope economies is flexibility of production processes. Goldhar and Jelinek (1983) identify these as a key issue in the effective use of new manufacturing technology.

Although the concepts of multiproduct costs and shareable inputs are useful for analysing the performance of firms in multiproduct industries, the treatment of those concepts in economic theory is weak. For example, Panzar and Willig (1981) adopt a mathematical approach to demonstrate '. . . an equivalence between economies of scope and the existence of shareable inputs . . .' (1981, p. 270). They continue, that there are economies of scope if and only if the capital service cost function (ie the costs of using a shareable capital input for two or more product lines) is strictly subadditive.

This result is hardly surprising. It amounts to a statement that *economies* of scope exist where the inputs to joint production of a set of products cost less than those required for equivalent separate production. If this is not a tautology, it is very close to one.

More importantly, the theory is misleading. Economies of scope are not achieved if costs of production are not 'strictly subadditive'. In the early stages of joint production, for example, investment costs would be higher – even to the extent of appearing as short term *diseconomies* of scope. Analysis of investment costs based on a longer term perspective would reveal a very different assessment – ie forward thinking and planning to reap the essential benefits of reduced costs in multiproduct operations.

As it stands, the theoretical literature on economies of scope offers only limited guidance for this analysis of the TSE industry. However, the concepts of excess capacity, shareable inputs and flexibility in production processes, have been used below to identify the major sources of cost saving in multiple production.

Economies of scope: the use of excess capacity

The concept of 'excess capacity' in production is not straightforward either in theory or practice.

In theoretical terms, the definition of excess capacity requires assumptions to be made about the 'optimal' use of factor inputs (both capital and labour), objective factors such as the actual demand for final product output, the nature of production as a single or multistage process, the rate of change over time of productive capacity, and subjective factors such as attitudes to risk and the time horizons of decision-makers within the firm.

In the real world the definition of excess capacity must take account of decision-makers' perceptions of current and future product and process technologies, their expectations of future demand for product output and, indeed, their own 'capacity' for production management. Such subjective factors found early expression in economic analyses of investment and innovation, for example, as the 'propensity to save or invest' in Keynes's *General Theory* and as 'animal spirits' in Schumpeter's account of the dynamics of capitalism.

It is clear that excess capacity can only be defined in relation to some notion of 'normal' capacity. The problem then is to find workable definitions of what is normal capacity at the firm, plant, process and sub-process levels. For example, if a firm has just completed an investment programme in PABX production facilities – based on expectations of rising demand for PABX products – it will presumably have excess capacity until actual product demand rises to the expected normal level. By contrast, if a firm has facilities set up for the production of outdated products – for which demand is falling below the 'normal' level – this too will have excess capacity but the competitive implications would be different.

In the former case, excess capacity would be an asset, offering opportunities to obtain economies of scope for example through diversification into related products based on similar technology. In the latter case, excess capacity would be a liability, reflecting perhaps the constraints of inflexible production methods in conditions of technological change.

Real-world production normally involves a number of tasks (ie sub-processes) – product design and development, component manufacture, product assembly, testing, packaging and so on. If production is seen simply as a single-stage process, 'capacity' can only be judged in relation to final product output. However, if production is disaggregated into its sub-processes, it becomes possible to identify excess capacity – and thus potential economies of scope – within *parts* of the production process. Such dis-aggregated analysis of production can take account of the specific techniques and machines used within the plant, rather than rely on a generalised description. Once again, excess capacity in sub-processes (for example as a result of the use of automatic component-insertion equipment) may be an asset or a liability, depending on the range (scope) of feasible alternative product-manufacturing uses for that stage of production and the level of demand for their services.

Excess capacity is also related to indivisibilities in factor inputs to production. These inputs include capital equipment, capital services, raw materials and components, and labour services. In each case, excess capacity within a given time period would result from a mismatch between a firm's demand for an input and the available scales of supply of that commodity or service. This may occur in two ways. Firstly, the only available unit quantities of an input may be larger than the firm would require for 'optimal' production; the firm may have no option but to purchase high-capacity machines for some particular task. Secondly, the supply of an input may not be adjustable downwards in the short term; it may be difficult or undesirable to make labour redundant, capital equipment may not be disposable, raw material and component bulk-purchasing contracts may be inflexible. Each of these rigidities would represent a barrier to market exit – a problem assumed away by Panzar and Willig (1981). Similarly, the overall utilisation of inputs for production may not be adjustable in the short term.

Excess capacity is related to the scale of production at the firm, plant, process and sub-process levels. Indivisibilities are central to the relationship between economies of scale and scope. Where excess capacity is a potential asset, scale and scope economies are complementary; where excess capacity is a liability, there is a trade-off (at least in theory) between economies of scale and economies of scope. The relationship between scale and scope in particular contexts depends on the nature of the manufacturing process and the firm's capacity to manage its own productive potential. It would clearly be unrealistic to assume that managers have 'perfect knowledge' and always use 'best practice' organisational techniques.

Economies of scope: shareable inputs

A second general source of economies of scope is the use of inputs which may be shared between two or more product lines. Input sharing may occur in two ways. Firstly, the capacity of an input – for example capital equipment used for component assembly – may be used up through the production of a number of different products. Parts of the input may be allocated to product lines on a time-sharing basis, for example where a flexible manufacturing system is used for batch production; or on a space-sharing basis, for example, where factory buildings are used to accommodate several product lines. The sharing of exhaustible inputs is closely related to the use of excess capacity.

Secondly, some inputs may be shared in such a way that their capacity is not exhausted, at least within broad limits. Non-exhaustible inputs are those that display some of the characteristics of public goods. In the theoretical literature, these are called quasi-public inputs or local public goods (Radner, 1986, p. 5) since their public availability is limited to the firm which uses them or the capital service supplier which controls them. Examples of quasi-public inputs include most forms of information and knowledge (notably R & D results), sales and distribution networks where the same network is used for a variety of products, communication facilities and some aspects of management such as strategic and personnel functions.

The distinction between exhaustible and non-exhaustible inputs to production is not rigid. Inputs with different technical and economic characteristics may be exhaustible to differing degrees, or within different limits. For example, information that is freely available within a firm may be less exhaustible than the capacity of the sales network to handle additional products. However, if such quasi-public-domain information is only available from on-line systems with limited access facilities, the position could be reversed: available capacity for gaining access to information could be exhausted more quickly than the capacity of a sales network to handle additional products. In practice, the ways in which economies of scope can be achieved from the uses of shareable inputs will depend on the particular characteristics of inputs and their uses in production. The degree to which inputs can be shared in a firm's production activities will, therefore, be an empirical question rather than a matter of logical necessity.

Economies of scope: flexibility of production processes

A third general source of scope economies is the use of flexible rather than fixed or rigid production processes. Flexibility in this context goes beyond equipment technology, although the characteristics of process equipment are undoubtedly important. Flexibility of management and operating procedures, and the adaptability of labour must also be considered. That is, achieving economies of scope through the exploitation of flexible production systems requires more than just the solution of engineering problems; it requires informed, skilful management.

Although production flexibility may often by closely related to the use of excess capacity or shared inputs, these three general sources of scope economies are distinguishable. Consider, for example, computer-based process technologies such as flexible manufacturing systems, robots or automated test equipment. These may be operated as a shared input, say between product batches. They also offer economies of scope by changing the range of products that may be feasibly produced. Flexible production technology widens the potential scope of the firm which uses it (Kaplinsky, 1984, pp. 70–1). As Goldhar and Jelinek put it: 'computer-based process technology sharply questions the established logic of production' (1983, p. 143). In particular, they contend that economies of scale – a widely accepted attribute of established rigid forms of production – are being over-taken by the potential of new technologies to offer economies of scope: 'effi-ciencies wrought by variety, not volume' (Goldhar and Jelinek, 1983, p. 142).

In a general sense, flexibility of production techniques underlies all sources of scope economies. Rigid, inflexible forms of production, using highly specialised equipment, cannot offer economies of scope even when excess capacity can be identified. At best, they allow for more production of the *same* product type, rather than the use of excess capacity for production of *different* product types. Similarly, flexibility in production logically includes the sharing of inputs. Sharing an input between two or more product lines implies that the input is flexible or general-purpose in use to some degree.

Flexibility is a necessary but not a sufficient condition for economies of scope in production. It is an essential aspect of *usable* excess capacity and shareable inputs, and it is a determinant of the potential for scope economies that may be achieved by the firm.

Dimensions of scale and scope in manufacturing industry

Scale economies in production

In order to analyse economies and diseconomies of scale in the TSE industry, it is necessary to identify the types of operations in which such economies may be realised, ie the sources of scale economies in production. It should be noted that in analysis of real industries there can be no assumption of constant and best practice technology throughout the firm or plant. Changes in technologies and their implications for costs must be taken into account in any empirical analysis of scale economies. Within the production environ-ment, potentially the prime areas for economies lie in specialisation and divi-sion of labour, indivisibilities and the economies of increased physical dimensions.

In this analysis, scale is conceived as the quantity of output within a given period of time. This is not the only way of viewing the potential costs and benefits of size though it is the most usual.

Seven aspects of scale economies in production are discussed below:

1 The length of production runs.
2 Technical economies of scale.
3 Managerial economies and diseconomies.
4 Scale of R & D.

5 Pecuniary economies of scale.
6 Dynamic scale economies: learning effects.
7 Technological change and economies of scale.

In each case, the concept of size or scale is open to interpretation; scale is not a one-dimensional issue.

1 The length of production runs

Separate from the issue of rate of output (number of items per unit time) is the planned total output of a production run, which can be a source of different economies. In production runs where a large element of cost involves fixed initial costs, length of run at a given scale will be significant. Hay and Morris (1979) give the example of book printing where typesetting is the major cost and so total volume is more significant than rate of output. Associated benefits of specialisation and learning are also achieved over long runs.

Usually length of run is regarded as synonymous with scale of plant, but the two may in some cases be distinct. A large plant producing items requiring little initial fixed cost may achieve significant economies not from long runs but rather from large numbers. Similarly economies of long runs may be achieved by small plants dedicated to very limited product ranges. However in those cases where the period of demand and length of run are not equal, additional costs may be imposed by the holding of inventory of finished stock.

In the TSE industry such economies may be possible in the case of particular components (e.g. plastic mouldings) although the initial costs as a proportion of total output are likely to be insignificant for even relatively small scale plants.

2 Technical economies of scale

Economies that are realised as a consequence of specialisation and reorganisation within the production process may be termed 'technical economies of scale'.

Increasing the scale of production allows a reorganisation of tasks through changes in the division of labour. Thus individual skills may be better utilised or, by 'routinisation', particular tasks may become easier for employees to carry out. Hence unit costs will be lower. The use of machines will also benefit from specialisation as they become dedicated to particular functions, thereby possibly reducing flexibility but increasing efficiency. Consequently 'down time' when retooling takes place will be reduced, leading to a more efficient use of assets.

However, these benefits will be limited by the extent to which product manufacture or assembly can be subdivided. With technical and design improvements in telephones, for example, the assembly process has been greatly simplified with a drastic reduction in the number of components to be assembled. This is typified by the use of integrated circuits (ICs) rather than discrete components. In this case, scale economies may be determined at a point in the assembly process where a specific machine is used, for example, for inserting components in a printed circuit board. At such a point, a number of individual production lines may merge, with each supplying inputs to the specific machine and assembling outputs from it.

In production, there also exist indivisibilities – particularly in 'lumpy' capital – as certain machines are only available in specific sizes or scales. For example, if a machine has a design capacity of 100,000 units per year at three-shifts operation then production facilities will tend to be organised around that size. A firm requiring a number of machines for a range of processes may need to achieve a scale which is the lowest common multiple of the outputs of all machines to be fully efficient. Thus if a particular machine requires an input of a specific sub-assembly at the rate of three times the throughput of the machine producing that sub-assembly, then the numbers of machines employed would need to be in proportion in order to avoid surplus capacity or bottlenecks. Processes which have scale requirements out of all proportion to the size of the firm may need to be sub-contracted out to another firm that could supply those services to a number of production activities.

However, there may be other reasons why such activities are retained in-house. These may be found within vertical integrated firms where a specific component is produced at a larger scale than the downstream activity requires. The component subsidiary may also seek to sell its output of components to third parties elsewhere. A similar argument would apply to a machine undertaking a particular process, where the cost of shipping part-finished goods to a subcontractor for a particular action may or may not be lower than the firm purchasing and then having to under utilise a large capacity machine. In this way, transport or transaction costs within and between firms are key elements in the viability of achieving technical economies of scale.

Another aspect of the large-capacity-machine argument is that a firm may seek to scale up a machine to seek additional savings. Thus, particularly in flow processes, a larger machine may have a much higher additional capacity than the required investment. This for example could be related to the changing 'ratios of containers'. (The volume of a container increases more rapidly than the surface area. Hence a pipe or tank of double a given capacity will require less than double the material in its skin, and so will presumably lead to a lower per unit cost in capital.)

It is also possible that the additional loads placed on the machine may require qualitative as well as quantitative changes, and scale economies may not be available over more than a limited degree of scaling up (Gold 1981). However, it is not anticipated that this aspect of scale economy is available to all TSE firms, due to its inapplicability to assembly operations, but it could be relevant to some aspects of component production.

A final issue relating to technical economies of scale is economies of massed reserves. Consider a production line composed of a number of discrete machines acting on a product in a fixed order. Clearly if one machine breaks down there will be a break in production at that point and subsequent machines will also need to stop. To avoid this requires stock-in-hand at all stages of the manufacturing process. This imposes an additional (investment) cost on production. If, however, a number of similar production lines run in parallel then the same stocks can be shared between several lines. Indeed, if there are a large number of lines then a break in one may be covered within limits by small changes in the rates of production of the other lines. Reallocation of part-finished goods between lines would enable all other machines to continue working with only very small increases in costs. The disruption costs of downtime caused by machine failures would be proportionate to the increase of the number of lines in operation. Simple arithmetic will demonstrate that the loss of one line out of five for a given period will impose lower disruption costs than the loss of one line out of three. However, in complex manufacturing processes, it is quite possible that marginal disruptions to production could impose disproportionately large costs, due to the difficulty of reorganising large numbers of operations.

3 Managerial economies and diseconomies

A separate range of scale-economy issues relate to managerial and other non-production activities due to organisational specialisation. If costs in real firms are considered as the total cost of participating in a particular activity, then this will entail the addition of not only any specifically relevant non-production costs but also some proportion of overheads carried by the organisation as a whole (for example non-specific corporate advertising). Much of the literature on diseconomies of scale refers to rising costs due to the 'pyramiding of management' (Penrose 1959, Bilas 1967). Clearly, in a firm-based analysis, all these potential costs must be taken into account.

Managerial economies of scale also include the cost effects of indivisibilities in particular departments and specialisation of function. In some respects, the benefits of scale may be less in terms of narrowly defined immediate cost efficiency than in *effectiveness* which leads to benefits being felt elsewhere in the organisation. For example, the increased effectiveness of a separate marketing unit (which is not available to a smaller firm) may be more important to the firm achieving further scale economies in manufacturing than in reducing costs in administration.

Managerial diseconomies are frequently cited as the main reasons for increasing costs as firms grow to very large size. Evidence of such upturns in the cost curve is notably absent (see for example, Penrose 1959 and Mansfield 1980). However, in a dynamic situation, large size may lead to failure by the firm on an industry scale curve that is falling away over time due to technological change. Writing nearly 60 years ago, Robinson (1931) discussed the problem of organisational ossification and whether large inflexible firms may be surpassed by smaller adaptable firms. Also, in relation to production investment, Robinson suggests that the lumbering giant may choose to optimise current least-cost scale and purchase specialised equipment, whereas a smaller competitor may trade short-term cost advantages for versatility in order to reduce future change-over costs. If this decision is in effect a consequence of managerial structures, diseconomies may be incurred as short-term savings are preferred at the expense of long-term competitiveness.

4 Scale of R & D

Research and development (R & D) is another field in which economies of scale may be realised. However, such economies will vary in importance according to the role that R & D plays in the competitive environment and according to the requirements of that R & D effort. In a new industry populated by small firms where R & D thresholds are low, scale economies due to R & D are not likely to be significant. As the industry matures and the basic science is understood, R & D will become more sophisticated and hence will require substantial investments to achieve some technological advance.

At this point, costs of research equipment, requirements of specialist staff and the growing number of personnel required to advance research sufficiently rapidly will raise opportunities for economies of scale within the R & D unit. In addition, substantial market entry barriers will be raised, in the form of thresholds below which R & D is not feasible (Freeman 1974, Mueller and Tilton, 1969). The logical conclusion of this argument of diminishing returns in R & D is that only large firms can meet the demands for resources (Galbraith 1952, 1972).

Above the threshold level another feature of R & D expenditure by firms indicates opportunities for economies of scale. If R & D is seen as a cost which is in part fixed (the threshold level) but also in part variable, then with larger sizes of firm the cost can be amortised over a large quantity of production. Analysis of firm size and R & D expenditure shows expenditure increasing more rapidly with size up to a point where, presumably, size of firm allows for additional forms of R & D to be undertaken. However, in the largest size groups, investment falls as a proportion of turnover as scale rises (Kamien and Schwartz, 1975). Thus the very largest firms seem to achieve economies of scale through more effective deployment of R & D expenditure.

Evidence from the telecommunications industry shows that in the case of public switches, for example, there is a level of R & D investment in absolute terms that is required to develop a product and this is rising for each generation. More specifically, with R & D costs in excess of $1 billion for the current generation of digital exchanges and a world market of only $14 billion in 1986, a supplier needs at least 10 per cent of that market to generate adequate returns over the life of the product (*Economist*, 1987). If the threshold is rising, this implies not only that a degree of scale is needed even to participate in the market, but also that the cost of R & D embodied in each unit of output will fall as scale rises. It is important to establish whether these trends are similarly evident in the subscriber equipment sector.

5 Pecuniary economies of scale

Another important area of potential cost reduction is that of pecuniary economies of scale, notably through bulk purchasing of inputs. A very large customer may be able to secure lower prices for components than a smaller firm and hence reduce the cost of inputs into the production process. This can come about in a number of ways. The component supplier may be able to realise economies from a large production run which can then be passed on in lower prices. The purchaser may also be able to exert monopsonistic power on the supplier to reduce immediate financial profits in return for security from continuity of orders. This power-dependency relationship may be stretched further with the supplier becoming locked into the large firm and, in turn for lower prices, receiving technology and capital from its customer to enable it to achieve low costs.

In the TSE industry the most important type of input component affected by such issues is likely to be the integrated circuit component (IC). In this case it is certainly true that minimum scale demand or order requirements exist for certain categories of device, and so large orders will be necessary and may result in some price discount. The power-dependency issue may also emerge, but it may not be straightforward; in some cases, TSE manufacturers are smaller than their component suppliers.

The large firm may be able to procure other inputs such as finance for new investments at lower cost than small competitors. Robinson (1931) suggests that larger firms may secure both a higher absolute level of borrowing and lower interest rates on the basis of lower risks. They also may have a wider range of options in terms of the different capital markets they may choose to approach and they may benefit from international differences in interest rates between national markets. However, in contrast, it is noted by Miller (1977) that the benefits of scale in terms of productivity and profitability may be in part passed on to the workforce in higher wages. It could by hypothesised that large firms may have to contend with more organised labour, and that unionisation will lead to higher wage demands. In some cases higher salaries may be paid to prevent unionisation occurring or to limit its extent, in order to achieve flexibility in other areas of labour relations such as demarcation.

6 Dynamic scale economies: learning effects
Large scale allows greater efficiency through division of function, so simplifying tasks. Related to this are the benefits arising from experience and learning by the workforce. With repetition comes speed and accuracy and hence greater productivity, as quantified by Alchian (1963) in the aircraft industry. Learning effects are not, however, restricted to labour-intensive sectors; Baloff (1966) identified benefits in capital-intensive plant due to the improvement of cognitive skills of the operating engineers. Baloff also points out that the benefits diminish and then die out after a particular level of cumulative output, although the rates of learning vary widely even for similar industries and products.

Gold (1981) and Silberston (1972) on the other hand, are critical of the inclusion of learning as an element of scale economies. Empirical studies may attribute improvements to accumulated experience or 'learning', but the simple case of repetition of a task will yield some rapid improvements, after which the method of performing a task is made habitual and improvement is not forthcoming. Longer-lasting effects are likely to emerge both from external factors (relating to quality and prices of inputs and competitive pressures) and from internal factors (such as the firm's product history, design, technology, organisation, and labour). In these cases 'learning' is still an appropriate description for a complex dynamic process but it is distinct from simple manual repetitive experience.

The relationship between learning and scale is therefore unclear. Although not necessarily exclusive, the two issues may be considered independently.

7 Technological change and economies of scale
One of the key assumptions of neoclassical production theory – based on statics or at best comparative statics – is that technology is constant and is of 'best practice'. Hence scale curves must be redrawn for each technology as a consequence of differing production functions. In practice this is clearly not feasible as all plants use slightly different technologies even if only in terms of differing organisational forms for different scales. In a firm, plants are of an assortment of vintages and hence technologies; they manufacture a range of differing products, particularly in rapidly changing sectors such as telecommunications; and they are subject to considerable variations in factor prices and qualities. Simply to compare costs between a number of plants without consideration of these issues is not to compare like with like.

Empirical research may encounter difficulties with differing types and levels of technology, unless account is taken of how this affects costs and what relationship it may have with size. The impact of technological change through product sophistication, especially where R & D costs are high, requires large-scale production to recoup investments. Innovation may also lead to significant simplification of products in manufacturing terms, reducing the number of tasks involved in assembly, for example by replacing complex sub-assemblies – requiring the assembly of discrete components – with a few ICs.

Two main technological issues are related to economies of scale. The first is that new technology can increase flexibility and so potentially undermine existing scale economies based on rigid techniques. Mature sectors may then be transformed through improved products and increased customisation thus undermining the established mass-production technologies (Abernathy et al 1983). As Ames and Rosenberg (1963) discuss within the context of technological change in national economies, pioneering or rapidly changing technology begets a proliferation of standards and specifications. The high levels of uncertainty created hamper the development of new economies of scale which do not appear until the technology matures and markets become stable.

The second issue is the cost of technology (whether in terms of processes or products) and the requirement to amortise costs over production runs. Do firms need to be large to use new technologies? Does technology encourage largeness? Or does largeness contribute to stagnation and risk-averse attitudes to new technologies? Finally do the disadvantages of small firms in the face of scale economies lead to demands for innovation to overcome these barriers?

Scope economies in production

This section relates the three general sources of scope economies – excess capacity, shareable inputs and flexibility – to the major aspects of real-world production. Five aspects of production are discussed briefly below:

1 Manufacturing-process technology.
2 Flexibility of product design.
3 Utilisation of material inputs.
4 Organisation and management.
5 Flexibility of marketing.

1 Manufacturing-process technology

Manufacturing-process technology is directly related to three aspects of product manufacturing. Firstly, the technology is embodied in the design of capital plant and equipment. This determines the technical limits to the range of functions that particular machines can perform. Automated insertion equipment, for example, is specifically designed to populate printed circuit boards with a limited range of electronic components; it cannot perform other operations. Secondly, manufacturing-process technology requires inputs of direct labour skills to make it usable. Although these specific inputs may vary in different contexts, some specialised labour will always be required, if only at supervisory levels. Thirdly, manufacturing process technology includes the methods used to organise capital and labour inputs in manufacturing.

Productivity may often be improved by organising the same capital equipment and the same labour in different ways. For example, in their paper on group technology, Hymer and Wemmerlov (1984) discuss the advantages of cellular manufacturing rather than job-shop or flow-shop organisation. These differing arrangements of equivalent capital and labour illustrate the benefits to be gained from the 'methods' aspect of manufacturing technology.

The potential for economies of scope in manufacturing depends on the flexibility of all three aspects of manufacturing process technology.

Firstly, the machines used by the firm must have the technical capacity to perform operations required for more than one product. On the one hand, machines which perform general purpose operations – drilling, turning, milling, paint spraying and so on – may be suitable for use in those operations in a wide variety of production process lines. General-purpose robots are perhaps the most flexible of such machines. On the other hand, machines which perform specialised functions may be reset for similar operation in closely related product lines; for example, automatic insertion equipment might be reset to handle differently sized integrated circuits or circuit boards for the production of computer rather than PABX hardware involving different component configurations. At this technical level, achieving economies of scope does mean solving engineering problems raised by the characteristics of specific types of capital equipment.

Secondly, widening the scope of production through exploitation of available technology has implications for the firm's demand for labour. The pattern of demand for labour of different types will depend both on the uses to which capital equipment is put and on decisions about how to organise production processes. For example, Hymer and Wemmerlov (1984) suggest that the use of cellular manufacturing technology with its capacity for wide-scope operation, requires higher levels of skills than established traditional forms of production. Yet changes in product design – for example in the assembly of telephone handsets – may reduce the required level of skills (and hence cost) of labour. Utilising the full potential range of process technology is likely to mean, therefore, changing the firm's skill distribution of labour – either through more training or through 'deskilling'.

Thirdly, the methods used to organise capital and labour in production need to be 'flexible' if economies of scope are to be achieved. Where machines are put to a variety of uses, so servicing different product lines, new manning labour arrangements may be required. If a machine is used to produce five different items instead of just one, it is quite possible that *more* labour (or more skilled labour) would be required to operate it. Maintenance would become a more complex task and the organisation of the machine's use would increase demands on managerial capacity. In such a case, economies of scope might be realisable only by increasing the proportion of labour (or labour quality) to capital.

2 Flexibility of product design

The second aspect of manufacturing which offers potential economies of scope is product design. In this context, product design refers to all parts of the design process from R & D through to production engineering. Effective design means taking account of both the desired characteristics of *products* for the user (features, reliability, appearance and so on) and the characteristics of available *manufacturing technologies*. For the producer, for example, design choices about how telephone components are to be assembled must take account of the costs of product assembly; simpler construction with fewer parts means lower unit manufacturing costs, but it may also require greater initial investment in product design and problems with security of supply of components (due to there being fewer suppliers of specialised components).

The balance between design and manufacturing costs depends on both the scope and scale of production.

In principle, R & D activities in multiproduct firms offer potential scope economies. R & D is essentially about the discovery or generation of new knowledge or information which may then be used for the production of other goods and services (see, for example, Freeman, 1974). That information is a 'quasi-public good', a non-exhaustible, shareable resource that may be freely used within a firm for the design of perhaps many different products. Clearly, the range of use of R & D information will depend on the content of that information and the nature of the products under development. Information about the design of closely related products (for example telephones and key systems) is likely to be more shareable, and hence offer greater scope economies, than that pertaining to more disparate products (for example telephones and other consumer electronic goods such as televisions).

The usefulness of R & D information relates to an important aspect of product design in the TSE industry: standardisation.

Firstly, the design process itself may be partly standardised through the use of computer-aided design (CAD) technology. The purpose of CAD technology is to increase the effectiveness of the designer through the provision of 'tools' of greater range and efficiency than manual techniques. The use of CAD technology allows consistent (standardised) design methods to be applied to different products, in so far as the design information (e.g. electronically stored drawings of components and products) may be *reused* for new product development. (Kaplinsky (1984, ch. 3) provides an excellent account of the history and economics of design-automation technology.)

Secondly, economies of scope may be gained through the use of the same components in different products. For example, there may be significant cost savings to be made by assembling the same components into a number of different telephone products. (This may be so even if the simpler models are deliberately 'retarded' or degraded so as to disallow the product user access to all of the facilities potentially provided by the component.) These cost savings are closely related to economies of scale, notably through the bulk purchasing and mass production of the same components. However, if standardisation is pushed too far, diseconomies of scope may result. Multiproduct firms which operate in conditions of rapid technological change, such as those in the electronics and telecommunications sector, face the danger of overcommitment to large-scale rigid forms of production. That rigidity can be caused by inappropriate use of standard components just as much as by inappropriate process technologies.

Achieving economies of scope through flexibility of product design may mean, therefore, pursuing *optimal* rather than *maximal* strategies for product-design standardisation.

3 Utilisation of material inputs

A third type of economy of scope involves efficient use of materials in production. In a general sense, any production process which does not fully utilise its material inputs must be inefficient. This type of inefficiency is reflected in either excess capacity of plant and equipment or the under utilisation or wastage of raw materials or component inputs. However, as argued above, the definition of excess capacity is not self-evident but depends on many non-engineering factors such as management awareness and firms' expectations of future economic conditions. Thus the identification of 'inefficient' uses of materials from observations of excess capacity in production alone should be treated with caution.

The potential for economies of scope from improvements in the use of raw materials or component inputs must be distinguished from general improvements in the efficiency of use of material inputs. Consider a manufacturing process in which one or more material inputs are not completely consumed, so that some material is wasted. In the strict economic and engineering senses, that manufacturing process is inefficient and – in theory at least – it will offer the potential for cost savings through improvements in efficiency.

Two types of efficiency improvements are possible here: waste reduction and waste recovery (where 'waste' becomes a 'by-product'). In the first case, the manufacturing process and/or product design may be altered to reduce the amount of a material input that is wasted as unusable scrap or lost into the environment. For example, a change in cutting patterns may reduce the amount of metal wasted when flat components are cut from sheet stock. Similarly, improved insulation may reduce wastage of heat; maintenance and tuning of power machinery may reduce fuel consumption. This first type of efficiency measure reduces unit costs but also reduces the potential for scope economies.

The second type of cost saving or efficiency measure also reduces unit costs but increases the potential for scope economies. This occurs whenever the wastage of inputs to one process or the by-products from it are used as inputs to a different process. By contrast with the previous examples, sheet metal left over from cutting operations could be recovered and sold for scrap or used as stock material for the fabrication of different components. Similarly, waste heat might be recovered and used as an energy input into a different production process. An example here would be the use of low grade heat from power stations to heat buildings and even to raise the productivity of fish farms. The direct use of by-products is perhaps most clearly seen in the chemical industry. For example, the synthetic production of polypropylene (a bulk plastic material) uses propylene – a by-product from oil refining – as its major input (Freeman, 1974).

In the manufacture of electronics and telecommunications products – particularly TSE – there are few if any significant material by-products. To this extent, one would not expect to find evidence of significant economies of scope derived from the utilisation of material inputs in the TSE industry. However, it is quite possible that TSE firms would achieve economies through waste reduction rather than waste recovery in product manufacture.

4 Organisation and management

A fourth aspect of production with the potential for economies of scope concerns the activities and functions of management. The organisation and management of production is not a costless activity. It is valid, therefore, to consider firstly whether the management function in multiproduct firms may be performed more cost-effectively than in single product firms; and secondly, whether existing management inputs to multiple production might perform a more effective range of functions.

Determining the relative costs of management in single and multiproduct firms may be difficult in practice. Conditions which have led to the presence of multiproduct firms in markets do not, typically, also encourage the development of single-product firms of equivalent scale. It is unlikely, therefore, that direct quantitive comparisons of management costs in different firms can be made in multiproduct industries.

While economies of scope in the management of multiproduct firms may be difficult to measure in practice, there is clearly a real possibility that such firms may incur managerial diseconomies of scope through the growth of bureaucracy. In any multiproduct firm, economies of scope can only be achieved if management considers – and acts upon – similarities and connections between products. As the size of a firm's product portfolio rises arithmetically, the number of potential connections between products rise exponentially. This means that management faces the exponentially costly task of reviewing potential sources of scope economies. Assuming (realistically) that the productivity of management can rise at most arithmetically, the quantity of managerial labour required to implement all possible scope economies must rise faster than the number of different products produced by the firm. In addition, as the number of managers increases arithmetically, their requirement for communication will increase exponentially – thus leading to the employment of yet more managers. The result, of course, is managerial bureaucracy.

In this way, managerial diseconomies of scope can arise both directly and indirectly. Arithmetic increases in product numbers lead directly to exponential increases in the cost of management required for economically rational decision-making (ie decisions based on consideration of all possible scope economies). If management is unable to consider all possible connections between products, at least some potential economies of scope – from whatever source – will not be achieved. The exponential growth of management would, therefore, result indirectly in scope diseconomies. Strictly speaking, these indirect diseconomies would arise from increasing opportunity costs of using inefficient production methods. That is, a firm which increases its product portfolio risks becoming relatively less efficient – and hence less competitive – through being less able to take up opportunities for cost-saving innovation.

5 Flexibility of marketing, sales and distribution networks
The final aspect of manufacturing which has the potential for economies of scope is the sale and distribution of products. The use of flexible modes of production to achieve economies of scope, through variety of products, has implications for firms' *marketing* strategy. As Goldhar and Jelinek point out, achieving maximum flexibility in production,

> . . . is of competitive value only if a company's marketing strategy emphasises customized products and frequent product changes, if its sales force is set up to handle such products, and if its R & D can provide a constant stream of product modifications and process improvements. (Goldhar and Jelinek, 1983, p. 144).

Similar considerations apply to the distribution of multiple products, where a company's distribution network may need to be changed to handle new products aimed at different types of customers.

Economies of scope are possible in marketing, sales and distribution activities to the extent that there is excess capacity to be used, or those activities are shareable inputs to production. Given the prevalence of payment by commission on sales, it seems unlikely that excess capacity would be identifiable at least among the sales force. However, it is very likely that additions to related product ranges (for example new telephone or PABX models) could be incorporated into existing marketing activities with little difficulty. Similarly, selling an expanded range of related products may be no more difficult (or costly) than selling the original range. Indeed, sales costs may actually fall if the expanded range of products starts to sell itself. However, these cost savings will depend crucially on the availability of appropriate sales networks and market knowledge.

Actual and potential scale and scope economies

Economies of scale and scope are not technologically or structurally determined; potential scale and scope economies are not automatically realised in practice. For example, if a given production process exhibits excess capacity, perhaps by being operated during only one shift out of three, it may not be practical to increase its capacity utilisation. Market demand may be insufficient to warrant greater output; established labour practices may be inflexible (for example through binding agreements between firms and their employees); or management may not be capable of organising increases in output through changes in the scope of production.

Similar barriers apply to increased utilisation of shareable inputs including, in some cases, the knowledge and skills of labour. Demarcation agreements and management inflexibility, for example, may limit the extent to which specific people may contribute to different areas of production. Software licensing agreements may have very similar effects on the utilisation of technically shareable computer-based technology.

In each area of production that offers potential economies of scale or scope (R & D, component purchasing, process technology, product design and so on), the achievement of cost savings depends on a number of strategic and operational decisions by management. Reducing costs necessarily means implementing changes in production. At the strategic level, long-term decisions must be made about major investment projects, commitments to existing products, the viability of new products, marketing of alternative outputs from existing production facilities, and even the firm's commitment to staying in a particular industry. It is quite conceivable, for example, that a firm in the TSE industry might choose to move into related but more profitable areas of the electronics and telecommunications sector. At the operational level, decisions must be made about changing work patterns (for example shift arrangements), material input supplies, product distribution, use of R & D results, communication patterns within and between parts of the firm, and so on.

The decision-making required to implement cost reductions in manufacturing is part of the function of management. Although changes in manufacturing may involve many people in many capacities, such changes are ultimately the responsibility of a firm's managers. Their practices, attitudes and abilities act as the final determinant as to whether potential economies of scope are realised in practice.

Scale and scope economies and firms' competitive strategies
Economies of scale and scope potentially affect the competitive position of firms and, thus, the strategic options available to those attempting to improve their position in multiproduct markets. These economies have direct relevance to the strategic behaviour of firms in the international TSE industry.

The cost structure of multiple production affects the ability of firms to enter multiproduct industries and to survive or succeed. Scope economies can act as both entry and exit barriers. The cost structure of multistage production may provide incentives for firms to integrate or 'internalise' their operations in a number of ways. However, the costs and benefits of integration vary; alternative strategic options must also be considered.

Firms attempting to enter multiproduct industries, in which economies of scope exist, face a problem: in order to compete against incumbent firms, new entrants must achieve better or similar cost profiles for products either in the short or long run. Given the existence of actual (or even potential) economies of scope in incumbent firms' production, new entrants would have to match these economies by engaging in comparable multiple production. Single-product firms, or those with a product mix that did not offer comparable scope economies, would not be able to compete with incumbent firms, unless they could achieve superior cost savings through very large-scale economies. Given that incumbent firms would also pursue such scale economies, economies of scope can act as a significant barrier to entry into markets. In practice, of course, potential entrants might choose to side-step the problem by producing for related niche markets or by engaging in more profitable activities elsewhere in other sectors.

A similar problem faces incumbent firms which currently enjoy economies of scope, but which try to exit from one or more specific product markets. For example, as the technology of TSE switching products changes, an incumbent producer may wish to exit from the market for small-scale PABX due to competition from other firms' sophisticated key-system products. In this case, short-run unit costs of producing the remaining products must rise, since the portion of total costs that was shared between, say, n products must now be shared between at most n−1 products. The greater the degree of scope economies achieved by the incumbent firm, and the smaller the portion of its product range it intends to retain, the greater will be the short-run barrier to exit from specific markets.

By definition, economies of scope must constitute entry and exit barriers in mulitproduct industries. For this reason, and for those discussed by Shepherd (1984), contestability theory (Baumol, 1982) is rejected here. Acceptance of contestability theory's stringent assumptions, notably that of costless entry and exit of firms from markets, would mean assuming away economies of scope. Such an assumption would be unwarranted in a study of the international TSE industry.

Fortunately, the literature on integration strategies of firms is more realistic in its treatment of market conditions. For example, Buzzell (1983) analyses the profitability of vertical integration strategies, and concludes by offering guidelines for cautious evaluation of the benefits and risks involved (1983, pp. 100–2). Buzzell's results suggest that the relationship between economies of scale and scope in manufacturing of specific products is an important determinant of the profitability of vertical integration. In particular, the commitments to given technologies implied by vertical integration may reduce the firm's flexibility, ie the ability to respond appropriately to changes in technology and market conditions (Buzzell, 1983, p. 94).

Horizontal integration is another strategic option for firms seeking cost savings through economies of scale and scope. However, simply buying into related or competing firms is not enough. Scope economies are achieved through the utilisation of excess capacity, the sharing of inputs or increased flexibility in production. Unless one or more of those conditions can be achieved, horizontal integration may lead to diseconomies of scope (or scale) through increased management costs. Horizontal integration can only be a viable option if the integrated firm is able to reorganise previously disparate production into a system which minimises excess capacity, shares inputs between product lines and retains flexibility.

Alternatives to integration strategies may offer firms the best chance of achieving economies of scope in practice. Joint ventures with other firms may provide opportunities for realising some of the benefits of integration without incurring the costs of ownership of other areas of production (Buzzell, 1983, p. 100). In particular, joint ventures and similar contractual arrangements may be limited to parts or aspects of production – joint R & D projects for example – that do not threaten the firm's ability to respond to market changes through product and process innovation.

Scale and scope dynamics

Economies of scale and scope in manufacturing industry are not static concepts. Cost savings through mass production or multiproduct manufacture are not predetermined. Rather, they depend on a range of factors which are known to vary over time and across different economic conditions. A key question for scale and scope analysis is under what conditions – if any – will the behaviour of these variable factors correspond to the predictions of existing production theory. For example, under what conditions can a firm respond to changes in the levels of demand for its products? Will 'best practice' technology necessarily be the same for all producers of a given size? Is it always economically rational for firms to invest in 'best practice' technology? What happens if they are unable to do so?

Existing production theory, on which the concepts of scale and scope economies are based, has one major flaw: it is a *static* theory of a *dynamic* process. The problem is not simply that parameters such as prices and quantities of capital and labour vary over time. It is that any static account necessarily assumes away all of the most readily identifiable dynamic features of modern manufacturing production.

This problem is illustrated in Figure 1.3 which describes some of the

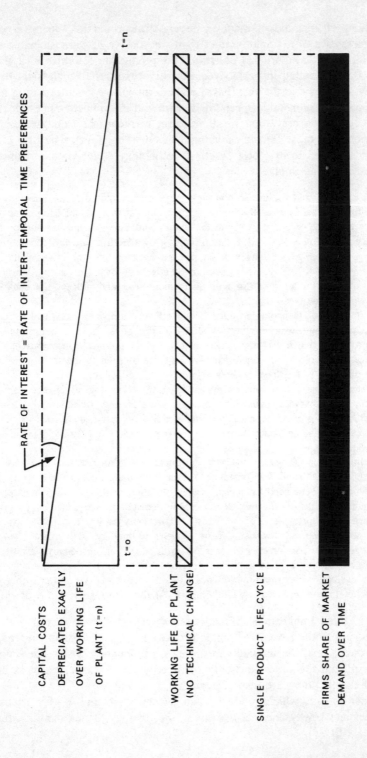

Figure 1.3 Assumptions of neo-classical theory

implications of assumptions made in neoclassical production theory. Even in
the simplest case of a single-product firm, the theory is not sustainable once
time is introduced. Figure 1.3 illustrates the production activities of a single-
product firm operating in perfectly competitive markets. Neoclassical theory
explicitly assumes that the firm has 'perfect' knowledge or information about
all technical and economic aspects of its own and its competitors' production,
and the conditions prevailing in all relevant markets (for example, that for
its products, and those for the capital and labour it employs). The firm is also
explicitly assumed to use 'best practice' technology which remains constant.
These assumptions imply:

- The cost of fixed capital (ie plant and equipment required in manufacturing) is
  written off exactly over the entire working life of that capital equipment.. (The
  very existence of interest rates in the theory implicitly assumes production takes
  place over time.) Rational decision-making by the firm and the competition it
  faces rules out either longer or shorter payback periods for investments.
- The working life of plant and equipment is exactly the same as the duration of
  market demand for the firm's product (ie product and process life cycles are
  assumed to be equal).
- 'Best practice' technologies must be specifically tuned to individual products;
  any technology which is not product-specific could always be refined and
  improved so that it was more efficient for a given product. This means that any
  process technology *must* have exactly the same lifespan as the specific products
  for which it is the 'best practice' method of production.
- As technology is constant during production, technological change can only
  occur when market demand for a product starts or stops (ie at $t = 0$ or $t = n$).
  Further, as process technologies are implicitly assumed to be specific to
  individual products, both product and process technologies must change when
  product demand starts or stops.
- Technological change – in both products and processes – is solely and
  completely determined by changes in consumer demand. No matter what new
  products are demanded by consumers the requirement for equilibrium in perfect
  competitive markets means that those new demands must be met (at $t = 0$) by
  a large set of producers. These firms must not only be able to produce whatever
  consumers demand (by using new product technology) they must also gain
  access to the 'best practice' means of doing so (by using equally new process
  technology). As soon as a market develops for a product that cannot be made
  (for example a perpetual-motion machine, a perfect chess program, or a TSE
  product that exceeds band-width limitations) the theory must break down.

Clearly, these implications of neoclassical theory do not accord with the
reality of production, even for single-product manufacturing. In the case of
multiproduct firms, the implied constraints on production possibilities raise a
more significant theoretical difficulty. Not only are the neoclassical assumptions unrealistic, they are also logically inconsistent.

Consider a firm which produces two products, A and B (for example,
telephones and key systems) at the same time, thereby having the opportunity

to realise economies of scope. Under the neoclassical assumptions, the firm would produce A and B using 'best practice' technology that is optimised for those two products. However, that production technology could not be 'best practice' since it would not be specific to either product; the technology employed to produce A and B would necessarily be a compromise. Yet the possibility of scope economies through multiproduct production of A and B suggests that this compromise technology might be *more* efficient than the best practice method available to specialised single-product firms producing just A or B. The problem here is that either the 'best practice' and 'most efficient' production technologies are not the same, or firms of a given size will rationally choose to employ different best practice technologies. As all firms in a perfectly competitive market are assumed to employ the same technology – the most efficient production method available – the neoclassical assumptions become contradictory when applied to multiproduct firms.

This theoretical problem means that neoclassical production theory must be rejected for the investigation of economies of scale and scope in the TSE industry. As narrow and contradictory assumptions were the cause of the problem, new and less restrictive assumptions must be employed.

Figure 1.4 illustrates some of the factors that are known to vary in the course of dynamic multiproduct production, such as that in the TSE industry. Firms do not have perfect information about all relevant technologies and markets but their products, processes and rate of output can change in the light of experience or improved information. This allows capital investment and depreciation costs to be related to the firm's degree of risk aversion, rather than being tied to a single 'rational' (ie perfect information) solution. In the same way, firms change their production plans in the light of changing market information about demand for products as the boundary between predictable and uncertain future demand changes with time.

By relaxing the unrealistic assumption of perfect information and thus allowing uncertainty, a less precise but more realistic view of firms' use of product and process technologies becomes possible. The firm described in Figure 1.4 is not constrained by an absolute need to use best practice technology or perish. Rather, it has a broad competitive incentive to employ a form of process technology that will still be efficient when changes in market demand – or product technology – require changes in the firm's product portfolio. The rational firm in these circumstances will be the one that 'hedges its bets' by attempting to optimise the efficiency of its operations over time, rather than trying to maximise short-term gains. The optimising firm also takes account of the possibility of future changes in process technology. This is shown in Figure 1.4 as a change in technology (at $t = n$) which lengthens the working life of the capital equipment employed. Unlike the simple neoclassical model (Figure 1.3), Figure 1.4 does not imply any direct correlation between changes in product and process technologies, nor does it impose restrictions on when such changes may occur.

40

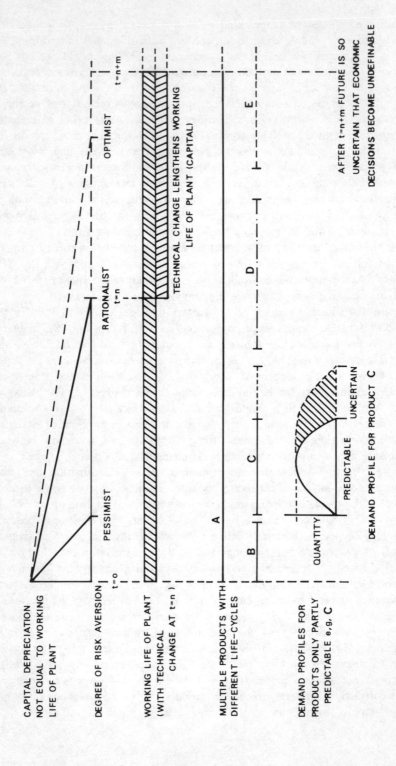

Figure 1.4 Scale and scope economy variables

Economies of scale and scope are necessarily dynamic concepts. Their availability and realisation by firms takes place over time during the course of production. Despite the shortcomings of the theory on which they are based, economies of scale and scope are clearly pertinent to the cost structures and hence competitiveness of firms in multiproduct industries. However, problems with existing production theory suggest that the nature of scale and scope economies – and their potential contributions to firms' competitiveness – requires detailed empirical investigation of real firms in multiproduct industries.

2 Manufacturing and Competitiveness

Introduction

Manufacturing forms one part of the activities of firms in the TSE industry. Complementary activities include R & D, marketing, sales, corporate finance and administration. These complementary activities support or are serviced by manufacturing – the principal area in which available technology is used to transform inputs into marketable goods.

Distinctions between manufacturing and a firm's other activities partly depend on the nature of the goods being produced. In particular, the boundaries between R & D and manufacturing, and sales and manufacturing may be blurred. For example, PABX products typically include software which may be either programmed after the hardware has been constructed, or embodied within 'firmware' components that are built into the product. In either case, the manufacture of PABX requires the creation of software. However, software development is essentially an R & D process, not a manufacturing activity. The task of creating new software is time-consuming, costly and difficult; the task of replicating existing software (ie its manufacture) is quick, cheap and relatively easy. While analysis of the costs of PABX production must take account of the cost characteristics of *all* components – including software development – analysis of manufacturing must be based on a more focused definition of activities and costs.

TSE products raise a second problem of definition – the distinction between manufacturing and sales activities. Telephones for example are much like conventional consumer products; they are designed, manufactured, tested then distributed. By contrast, not all PABX products can be sold to end users in such a straightforward way. Before a PABX sale to an end user is completed, the product must be installed on the customer's premises and then tested. (It is common practice for 'acceptance testing' criteria to be written into the conditions of sale for PABX and similar products.) Similarly, installed products may require 'debugging' or fine tuning – engineering tasks which are essentially the final stages of the production process.

'Manufacturing' is therefore taken here to refer to all activities that are required to transform inputs into goods available for sale. However this does not include the production of software and other information components (for example data, operating and maintenance manuals) which is part of the R & D function. Neither does it include on-site work at customers' premises required for the completion of an installation, even if that work is undertaken by the TSE firm itself. Custom or systems engineering is only considered here as part of 'manufacturing' to the extent that it involves physical product-fabrication activities. (Similar work undertaken by dealers or system houses, for example, would not be considered within TSE production or manufacturing.)

In a previous study of the TSE industry (Sciberras and Payne, 1986), the form of the manufacturing process was found to be a key factor in the competitiveness of firms. The success of TSE firms in achieving long-term pre-eminence over rivals depended crucially on their ability and willingness to manufacture products of appropriate quality in the most cost-effective way. Competitiveness is not a straightforward concept in this context. It depends on the quality and prices of products, firms' costs and profitability relative to rivals (BEQB, 1982) – factors which depend on the form, quality and costs of the manufacturing process. While manufacturing costs are affected by economies of scale and scope, the manufacturing process also involves other elements which affect the competitiveness of firms.

The production function

Production function theory suggests that labour and capital are brought together in an optimum combination to achieve low-cost production. In neoclassical economics, this is conditioned by a number of assumptions relating to the unitary nature of the production plant, the homogeneity of inputs and outputs and the availability of best-practice information about technologies and markets. Clearly, in efforts to achieve industrial competitiveness this simplification is of little analytic or prescriptive value. Firms however must make some estimate of manufacturing costs according to a balance of factor inputs, and attempt to pursue an optimum or acceptable combination within a particular period of time.

The assumptions of the neoclassical theory are inappropriate to the accounting task of the firm. Homogeneity of factor inputs, for example, is clearly inappropriate to labour. Materials are presumed to be of constant cost, quality and applicability. This is unrealistic. The purchase of factors is presumed to take place in open markets with unlimited availability; whereas, in reality such markets are segmented, differentiated, geographically defined, and factor costs are variable according to the size, status, ownership, and managerial competence of the firm.

The notion of best-practice technology throughout an industry, is also a problem for three reasons. Firstly, such information may be proprietary and withheld from access; secondly, the research process will impose costs on its acquisition; and thirdly there will be time lags in its availability for implementation for some firms.

Theory has also failed to deal adequately with technological change and manufacturing. There is little to learn from the production function about product innovation and manufacturing, as each function assumes a fixed homogenous product. New products require new factor relations (Rosegger, 1980). As products continually change in terms of design, function and cost:performance ratio, this aspect of competitiveness is effectively ignored in conventional analysis. Process innovations are generally defined as 'a change in input–output relationships that results in lower unit costs for the presumably unchanged output, even though input prices have remained constant' (Rosegger, 1980). Clearly, this presumes much and fails to match observable reality. Process innovations may not be primarily aimed at cost reduction, they will usually involve some change in the product, especially in assembly operations, and input prices cannot be relied upon to remain constant.

The assumptions about inputs in the model are also generally unsupportable. In the case of material costs – assumed to be a constant and hence excludable item – process change may have significant implications for quality and hence cost. The form of materials will change as products are often redesigned for new processes. Labour is assumed to be homogenous, but when labour displacement occurs during process innovation or even if number of employees remains constant or increases, the type of labour, their skills and remuneration, will change. New managerial techniques necessary to implement the new technology may also have significant impact on the structure of the labour force affecting costs and productivity.

Competitive strategy and manufacturing

Traditional economists have conceived of the technical organisation of production as a 'black box', bringing together labour and capital. Management scientists have considered manufacturing as one element in a strategy or game by the firm. The significance afforded to manufacturing, however, in relation to other elements of activity within the firm has until recently been low. It has only been since the overall relative market stability of the 1960s and early 1970s was overturned in the late 1970s and 1980s, that there has been a shift in the analytical view of business strategy away from the long-term, corporate level down to the detailed strategic manufacturing issues of individual businesses. The former emphasis on portfolio analysis and long-term investment optimisation was undermined by turbulent market change in what had been secure growing markets. With capacity rationalisation in many sectors and more intense competitive behaviour even in growing markets, the importance of successful short-term operations management appeared to take precedence over long-term strategic planning. This reflected the concern that failure to respond adequately on a short-term basis would mean that a firm had no long-term future in a sector. Hence any long-term strategic plan, it might be argued, would be undermined by short-term competitive pressures.

Competitiveness therefore became a much higher priority in the business environment embracing all aspects of the firm's operations. It is no longer adequate for business analysts to compare performance on simple criteria such as profitability and investment. Modern business strategy is concerned with making moves which confer advantage over competitors' positions, with the identification of the correct move being secondary to the ability to execute it at the correct time compared with the competition (PSI, 1986). This emphasis is now emerging in new studies of business history as well as prescriptive texts (for example De Lamarter's (1987) study of IBM and Pettigrew's (1985) study of ICI).

Michael Porter has advocated the need for a broad approach to competitive strategy which also takes cognisance of the detail of response. Porter's analysis begins with competitive relations within individual markets. The structural determinants of the intensity of competition in this context go far beyond simple rivalry with current competitors, to include the bargaining power of buyers and suppliers, and the threat of new entrants or of substitute products (Porter, 1980). The competitive firm must be able to interpret and respond to – for example – attempts by suppliers or customers to exert market power to change the terms of trade in their favour. This may be particularly threatening if it is a prelude to an attempt by the supplier or customers to integrate vertically. Alternatively, by changing the terms of trade a firm may reduce the level of value added attributable to its supplier or customers.

More recent work by Porter on establishing competitive advantage stresses the concept of the 'value chain' within the firm (Porter, 1985). The value chain represents the activities within the firm that collectively design, produce, market, deliver and support its product. They include *primary activities*, involved in the physical manufacture of the product and its subsequent sale, and *support activities* that underpin this: firm infrastructure, human resource management, technology development and procurement. Competitiveness can then be seen as the way in which the value chain is manipulated relative to that of competitors (as widely defined above).

Thus the overall competitiveness of the firm is determined by appropriate strategies for virtually all aspects of the firm's operations. The main elements with respect to manufacturing operations, can be summed up as product strategy, manufacturing strategy, operational strategy and human resource strategy (PSI, 1986).

Capital investment in manufacturing

Firms invest in manufacturing plant and equipment in order to reduce costs, to maintain or increase net revenue from product sales. Investment is required for new products, new processes or both. It is also required for the replacement of obsolete equipment and for the expansion of production capacity. As product and process technology develops, the viability of existing products and manufacturing processes changes. In conditions of technological change, the profitability of capital investment, and the firm's own ability to exploit the potential of its production facilities are not fixed but will vary according to the market behaviour of the investing firm's rivals. For example, investment in more efficient equipment for PABX manufacture may be very profitable under current or predicted conditions. If, however, a rival firm develops a technically superior product, manufacturing the original PABX model by *any* process – no matter how efficient – may no longer be competitively viable. Successful investment in manufacturing is, therefore, as much a question of overall competitive strategy as of efficiency.

It is important to distinguish between reductions in costs and increases in net revenue as reasons for manufacturing investment. Cost reduction – irrespective of how it is achieved – can only improve a firm's competitiveness in markets for established products where price levels are constrained. In order for cost-reducing investment to be effective, demand for products must be expected to be maintained long enough to cover the cost of the investment itself. If the firm expects demand for a given product to fall due to non-price competition from rival products, there may not be sufficient incentive to invest in more efficient manufacturing processes. However, 'optimal' investment does not necessarily mean adopting the lowest unit-cost production technology. There may well be an incentive to invest in plant and equipment to manufacture a more sophisticated product, even if the costs of manufacture – and the product's price – are higher than before. In this case, an expected increase in net revenue over a sufficient time-scale would warrant the investment in new capacity.

Investment decisions are central to a firm's manufacturing policy. The viability and rationale for capital investments are closely related to the firm's long-term plans for product development, marketing strategy and deployment of current and future technology. These issues are discussed by Stobaugh and Telesio (1983), who conclude that manufacturing policies must match product strategies; that these strategies must be dynamic, and that manufacturing policies must change over time – via the investment process – to remain appropriate.

The investment process is governed by a number of constraints, of which financial profitability may be the least difficult to assess. Although profitability is clearly a necessary condition for investment in manufacturing, it is not a sufficient condition for realising the benefits of investments in practice.

All non-trivial capital investments in manufacturing necessarily alter the pattern of tasks and activities within the firm. Changes in products or processes directly affect the activities of management and labour by requiring new sets of tasks to be undertaken in the production of the firm's output. Task performance requires skill, effort and appropriate experience, whether the task happens to be assembling new products, operating new machines or organising the use of new plant and equipment. Manufacturing investment may therefore affect the work of every member of a firm, from the managing director to the most junior apprentice. In view of the potential repercussions of investment decisions, non-financial factors play a crucial part in determining the viability of new products and processes.

The ability and willingness of employees to perform new tasks is particularly important here. Capital investment typically creates a need for new skills which may involve employee training; for example, how to assemble new types of telephones, how to operate new circuit-testing equipment, how to use critical-path analysis in planning the operation of flexible manufacturing systems, or how to structure the firm's accounting practices to accommodate new capital costs. In each case, skill shortages or lack of training of appropriate employees will constrain the viability of an investment project. Essentially, capital investment in the manufacturing process requires complementary investment in labour if it is to be successful. Instances of employee resistance to capital investment projects often reflect inadequate or inappropriate investment in people: unwillingness to cooperate may be a perfectly rational response by managers or shop-floor workers who perceive particular changes to their activities as a threat. Conversely, active cooperation by employees (at all levels) who perceive benefits from change (higher rewards, more interesting work, better working conditions and so on) may greatly enhance the viability of capital investment projects.

Capital investment in manufacturing must also overcome a number of organisational constraints. Firstly, corporate commitments to existing products must be taken into account. The design of new products and their method of manufacture may need to be compatible with existing technical standards (for example data-transmission protocols) even where more advanced design possibilities are available. If demand for old products remains high, it may not be viable for firms to force the pace of technological change by investing in plant and equipment for manufacturing radically new products. Secondly, commitments to existing capital equipment must be taken into account. Investment decisions require the benefits of new plant and equipment to be traded off against remaining amortisation costs on old capital, plus the costs of reorganising production including those of assessing product and process compatibility. Multiplant firms may reduce these costs by transferring or relocating out-dated capital equipment from a core manufacturing plant (this process typically involves exporting old capital equipment to plants in less-developed economies.) Thirdly, effective investment in manufacturing requires access to the appropriate technology *and* the means to utilise it. Here, the viability of an investment may be constrained by the availability of specialised labour, including management with sufficient technical knowledge to organise effective use of the new capital equipment.

Capital investment in manufacturing is necessarily a strategic activity of the firm. It involves long-term commitments to process technologies which may or may not accommodate future desired changes to product design. Similarly, current investment projects are constrained by the firm's previous strategic decisions.

The concept of a strategic approach to manufacturing *per se* has been claimed to have emerged as a response to the US productivity crisis of the early 1970s (Skinner, 1974). At that time Skinner introduced the concept of the 'focused factory', arguing that, by concentrating the activities of a factory on a narrow product mix and particular market, higher performance could be gained over broad-mission plants. The tightly focused factory would have lower costs due to its higher degree of specialisation, but this was secondary to its main advantage. This was that the factory would be easily directed to the particular task required to produce a competitive product.

In Skinner's view the plant that was a hodge-podge of compromises with regard to products, markets, delivery schedules and technologies, often with high overheads to coordinate these elements, would inevitably compromise on the competitiveness of its output. The focused factory would determine what was essential for its output to be competitive (cost, performance, delivery, quality) and direct its resources towards satisfying those specific focused objectives. However this does not necessarily imply separate dedicated factories, but could include plants within a plant with clear demarcation of tasks between them.

In effect Skinner argues that emphasis should be placed on simple scale economies, or very limited shared resources between closely related products, in contrast to the haphazard seeking of scope economies. The effect of this type of discussion has been, to some extent, a shifting of emphasis from economies of scale in large general plants to narrowly defined economies of scale in individual products. Thus a telephone-manufacturing facility reaping economies of scale would not be presumed to benefit from being combined with PABX manufacture in a yet larger, but more diverse, plant. However, more recent analysis of economies of scope – associated with the production of related products – conflicts with the notion of the focused factory.

Product design and process change

Product technological change either of an incremental or radical nature has a vital role to play in both cost reduction and differentiation strategies. Although it is traditional to view process change as instrumental in reducing costs, the potential benefits may not be realised without some change in product design. New automated assembly processes, in particular, will demand some change in product design to allow for ease of operation. The replacement of several components by one integrated device and the reduction of materials content or use of cheaper materials will also lead to cost reductions as a consequence of design changes (Porter, 1983).

Product-differentiation strategies rely upon high quality, additional features and custom design. Proprietary technology in the design may also be used defensively to inhibit subsequent sales by competitors through limiting system capability of products. For example, if a particular model of PABX requires certain advanced features on terminal devices then buyers will restrict their purchasing to the company that can supply those devices, usually the PABX manufacturer itself.

The role of product design in competitiveness can also vary over time. This depends upon either market pressures such as deregulation and improved consumer choice, or on technological opportunities as in the added features that may be available from new components or software. Currently the TSE industry is undergoing a phase of rapid technological change as both market and technological pressures direct firms towards this aspect of competitiveness. In particular, there has been a shortening of product life cycles as a consequence of market demands permitted by, and new opportunities arising out of, technological progression.

Swann's (1986) study of the microelectronic component industry found that 'quality innovation', the introduction of a new or improved version of an existing product, is a major competitive force in that sector. Although technological opportunities exist to develop higher-quality components, greater speed, reduced power consumption, increased reliability and capacity at reduced cost, the consumers of these products are lagging in their ability to make maximum use of this capability. For example, telephone-exchange manufacturers have resisted the use of state-of-the-art components for two reasons. Firstly, the requirement of extremely high reliability in electronic exchanges necessitates proven technology and long development times. Secondly, there is an unwillingness by the customers and manufacturers to make an installed base prematurely obsolete, because of government investment limits on PTTs, and because of manufacturing, design and operating difficulties in the transition from electromechanical to electronic equipment. However, despite this inhibition by some users, semiconductor firms are faced with a competitive environment in which benefits or improvements are rapidly cancelled out by competitors, yet failure to make those improvements leads to product domination by those same competitors.

Quality innovation in the TSE industry appears to be a newly emerging force, as previously closed markets begin to open up, simultaneously with technological opportunity. The potential for exploitation of the available technology remains huge and, despite attempts by some existing suppliers to protect an installed base from replacement, the competitive opportunity exists for innovative firms to initiate technological competition. The extent to which firms are responding to such opportunities can be seen from changes in product life cycles.

Automation

Kaplinsky (1984) identifies three main spheres in which automation can be applied in the manufacturing firm. These are design, the manufacturing process and coordination (or management and operation). In each sphere there are a number of potential areas for the application of information and communication technologies to increase productivity. At a more radical level of change, the 'factory of the future' concept would require the linking of all three spheres within a total automation strategy.

Within the design sphere, computer-aided design (CAD) technology has enabled the more rapid implementation of many routine tasks in the design process such as the production of designs and drawings with only slight variations on a common theme. This is secondary to being able, through automation, to produce designs which would not be possible or practical by manual means. For example, the increasing complexity of circuitry, particularly in IC design requires a very large number of logical tests to be made for each slight alteration in the circuit layout. Above certain levels of integration this can *only* be done with computer assistance.

CAD not only affects the design process quantitatively by easing the burden of frequent repetitions of draughting or logical testing, but also has a qualitative impact on the final product. Thus a CAD system may act as a optimising tool, not only with respect to tailoring the design for specific customers and applications but, more significantly, optimising performance and the ease and cheapness of production (Kaplinsky 1984).

As a consequence of these changes in the design process, CAD allows lead times for design work to be reduced. Thus response rates to new market opportunities, calls for tenders, and competitive products can be much more rapid. One illustrative case concerns a UK electronics firm wishing to supply a sub-assembly for an American defence contract. The US customer announced new design requirements in the evening. These were faxed by the local salesman to the UK for the beginning of the next working day, and the tender was redesigned, costed and specified using CAD. The ability to respond in less than one working day allowed the tender to be faxed back to the USA to reach the customer on the morning after the change to the specification. The UK firm received the contract. Even with the benefits of facsimile communications, such response times would not be possible using manual design methods.

The electronics industries have been particularly active in the adoption of

CAD as a pure design tool as opposed to the more common use for draughting. The complexity of circuitry both at component and board level has required automation to enable continued increases in circuit density and sophistication.

In the manufacturing sphere the degree of automation possible, and the extent to which this is achieved varies immensely due to a number of factors.

Firstly, the basic nature of the manufacturing process, and the types of operations carried out, establish the possibilities for automation. For example, chemical-flow processes are automated by necessity whereas forming, cutting and assembly operations in manufacturing may present a number of problems in the replacement of human skill by programmed machines. One area in which automation is particularly difficult is in the handling of work in progress and its positioning for subsequent operations. Automation of such complex integrated operations is often beyond the capability of all but very stable, specialised, high-volume manufacturing plants to implement.

Secondly, there are factors relating to the industry that influence adoption of automation techniques. If the size of firms, typical batch sizes and levels of profitability are low, delays may occur in the adoption of new process technologies. For example, the manufacture of cars is more automated than that of more specialised vehicles for agriculture, construction or defence. In the IT and electronics industries, it may be expected *a priori* that the manufacture of most production items such as telephones, personal computers and consumer electronics products (for instance televisions and audio equipment) would be subject to higher levels of automation than that of small batch or customised products such as PABX and defence equipment.

Thirdly, the adoption of automation is influenced by a number of firm-specific factors. Examples here include profitability, management awareness of the strategic benefits of automation, the degree of cross-subsidisation between products and between divisions, and inter-divisional standardisation. Awareness of the potential of automation may vary widely between different firms in an industry or sector. International variations in awareness – and adoption – of automation by firms may be strongly influenced by differences between nations' investment policies, tax structures and factor prices.

Labour in manufacturing

The variations in the attributes of labour are immense. Skills, experiences and cultural differences produce a labour force so diverse that (absolutely contrary to conventional economic notions) heterogeneity may be regarded as its distinguishing characteristic. The firm will require a specific mix of types of labour to combine with a particular capital investment. Increased capital intensity may lead to a new reduction in the overall number of employees, but with significant increases in particular skills. In this way, redundancy and hiring may coincide.

Different forms of labour will be priced according to training, skills, productivity and scarcity. Total labour costs therefore reflect types of skills as well as number of employees, with the highest costs falling in the non-production rather than direct manufacturing workforce. Indeed, as many firms now employ more people in white-collar than blue-collar operations, 'non-production' labour costs will be dominant.

Consider a TSE firm with one or more manufacturing operations in specific locations with existing workforces. The first option for the firm is to gain maximum benefit from those existing operations, either by manufacturing at lowest cost, or using other means of differentiation such as higher quality or performance. Decisions to change the labour force, either by changing in-situ skill composition, or by changing the locational distribution of manufacturing operations, necessarily involve more long-term objectives. Such changes will usually be initiated in response to changing conditions for competition and manufacturing rather than short-term variations in market demand for particular products. These major changes may require new investment in alternative locations, especially if expansion in new markets is involved. Restructuring within the industry – whether by the acquisition of additional capacity or selective closure – will often radically affect employment immediately, and in these situations a complex re-ordering of the spatial structure of production and occupation will take place (Massey & Meegan, 1979; Peck and Townsend, 1984).

The TSE industry has so far not exhibited as strong an international division of labour as other technology-based sectors such as semiconductors or consumer electronics, although there has been a recent growth of telephone production in the NICs. Most firms still retain much of their production in their domestic markets. However, increasingly, overseas investment is reflecting the desire to penetrate overseas markets, with local assembly being required in many countries to enable sales. Within countries, distinct regional production hierarchies are emerging, and the continued restructuring of the sector may lead to further national and international production hierarchies being formed.

Manpower issues can be viewed in two ways. One perspective would stress the direct economic consequences of buying labour at particular prices and its utilisation within the manufacturing process. The firm must then respond to cost and price changes by changing its expenditure on labour and consequently adjusting its utilisation by, for example, job shedding, deskilling, or skill polarisation. A second perspective would stress human relations management as a means of maximising the benefit to be gained from a specific investment in labour. Team working, quality circles, employee participation in decision making and training are all elements of strategies to optimise the use of labour.

A number of factors have contributed to pressure on firms for changes in their traditional manning practices. The effect of economic crisis since the late 1970s has reinforced pre-existing imperatives to improve productivity, partly by rationalising excess capacity (especially in older, high-cost facilities) and partly by changes in the labour process itself. One common approach to the problem has been to increase capital intensity in high-labour-cost locations, with a shift of certain labour-intensive activities to lower-labour-cost locations in peripheral areas, either within the national economy (rural areas, high-unemployment locations or subsidised regions) or overseas (particularly the newly industrialising countries of South East Asia). This trend however has been less noticeable in telecommunications manufacturing.

The need to increase productivity and cut labour costs, to withstand increased competition and volatility in markets and to cope with increased technological change all require increased flexibility from the workforce (Atkinson & Meegen, 1986). A framework developed at the Institute of Manpower Studies presents the different possible dimensions of such changes. Four main types of flexibility are identified:

- Numerical flexibility – the level of employment, with use of supplementary labour to meet levels of output above a certain minimum: part-time, temporary, casual workers, overtime.
- Functional flexibility – increased versatility of existing employees to permit redeployment between and within jobs. For example the reduction of demarcation and the emergence of the concept of the multiskilled operative.
- Distancing strategies or externalisation – replacing employment relations with commercial transactions through subcontracting, particularly for short-term capacity increases and non-core activities, for example security and catering.
- Pay flexibility – tailoring the reward system to support the numerical and functional flexibility above, for example through personalised pay scales instead of standardised rates.

The ability successfully to prosecute such strategies is vital to effective competition if labour is to be seen as a resource rather than a cost. Competitive advantage may depend upon being able to respond quickly to market opportunities and to introduce new organisational and technological methods into production at least cost. Corporate flexibility will determine success in the implementation of these changes.

Even with a 'flexible' firm there will still be a core of employees who will be relatively secure. Branton and Livingstone (1979) stress the importance of security as a corporate objective with regard to both external contractual obligations and internal control issues. Therefore, there are considerable incentives to avoid the problems of labour disruption and to establish security of labour supply for skills which are scarce.

Manpower policy can also be used as a positive competitive instrument. It appears that there are significant differences between firms in the effectiveness with which such policy is used. The creation of differentiation in labour management may yield competitive advantage. A given state of technological development will only be capable of being implemented by manpower, through the firm's managerial capability. The phenomenon of X-inefficiency, whereby the optimum use of technology and practices is inhibited by managerial problems, is the inevitable consequence of human fallibility. It is demonstrated historically wherever a firm improves its performance through changes to managerial practices.

Managerial literature of the *In Search of Excellence* genre focuses on the benefits to be gained from staff development, training, communication and interpersonal relations within the organisation. Emphasis is generally placed on the activities of engineers, managers and administrators – whether intentionally or not. The methods adopted generally relate to the passing of information and the improvement of such information flows. However, the best-practice managerial techniques can apply to both production workers and management staff: how they are motivated, how effectiveness can be increased and how they can contribute to improved competitiveness. Much literature focuses on the potential for conflict in the introduction of new technology, but little as yet explores the way competitiveness is achieved by firms using labour and other strategies in constructive harmony. Walton and Sussman (1987) stress the importance of human resource management in production with specific relevance to the introduction of advanced manufacturing technology (AMT).

This raises a number of issues that are to be covered in this investigation of the problems facing manufacturers wishing to implement manufacturing-based competitive measures.

- Production skills are important. The upgrading of such skills may be one factor associated with effectiveness in manufacturing. This is especially so if retraining includes combining maintenance or quality-control functions with assembly work. Deskilling may also occur, but it may not be the most effective way of achieving competitiveness.
- Changing emphasis on quality and inventory control within the manufacturing process may require greater functional integration and changes in both skill and attitude. Responsibility may be increased and identification of the production worker with the firm's objectives may also increase. This is a new departure for many firms with a hire and fire policy with may have led to conflict in the workplace in the past.
- Machine and functional integration, reduced inventories and the elimination of queueing requires a team approach on the part of the whole workforce with joint responsibility for problems. This has resulted in considerable changes in many aspects of work and poses considerable challenges for both the steady-state management of people as well as the more dynamic management of technological change in the workplace.

Quality and supplier relationships

Procurement and quality control have traditionally been viewed as low-level operational functions, divorced from the wider concept of competitive strategy (PSI, 1986). However the Japanese experience with total quality control suggests that the benefits of high quality in cost reduction and product differentiation can be considerable, especially when combined with other attempts to achieve competitiveness by product and manufacturing strategies.

The mainstream economic viewpoint has generally regarded the purchase of components and raw materials as market transactions, conditioned by prices and market structure (Casson, 1987). Casson suggests however that such transactions are increasingly being influenced by non-price factors, and that organisational innovations are radically changing the way in which supplier–user relationships are formed. The complexity of such relationships, with their requirement for continual two-way flows of information, in addition to the money–material exchange, leads to a need to examine these relationships with regard for their effect on competitiveness.

TSE product manufacturers depend on reliable supplies of components of specified quality. In the case of microelectronic components, even small variations in quality can have very significant effects on usability. No TSE manufacturer can afford to use sub-standard components in its products; a PABX which incorporated faulty ICs which only work 'most of the time' would not be a viable product! Similarly, reliable delivery of supply is very important. Many TSE components are highly advanced specialised pieces of technology, available only from a few suppliers. Firm-specific ICs, for example, may be produced by only one supplier. The greater the degree of specialisation of components, the fewer substitutes will be available and, hence, the greater will be the dependence of the product manufacturer on particular component suppliers. Equally, of course, the supplier may have few – even just one – customer for its output of components. In this case the relationship between supplier and customer (ie TSE firm) will be strategically determined. That is, each firm will examine the strategic significance of its relationship with its supplier/customer and will seek a non-market solution in those cases where risk is highest.

The economics of manufacturing can be adversely affected by the presence of faulty or low-quality components. In procurement therefore, the quality level must be a part of the decision process. Otherwise, savings made at that stage may be wasted by additional costs later in the manufacturing process. Additional costs which may be incurred due to components being less than 100 per cent usable can be expressed under three categories related to the three stages at which costs may be incurred: pre-assembly, assembly and post-assembly.

- Pre-assembly costs are costs attributable to the processing of goods inwards.

This includes transaction costs (encompassing administrative costs of returning stock identified as faulty), chasing up late deliveries and costs of holding inventory. These costs may be lowered by high-reliability deliveries, zero-defect supplies and 'just-in-time' (JIT) schedules.

● Assembly costs. Should faulty components reach the assembly stage, a number of possible problems could develop. The component may cause a jam or breakdown in the production process; a faulty sub-assembly may be produced which is either waste or requires remedial treatment; or a 'bug' may lie undetected in the sub-assembly to create a fault in a later test stage or else in use.

● Post-assembly costs. Low-quality components may get through the production process undetected, achieving normal functionality on delivery, but the reliability and durability of the equipment may be compromised in the long term, leading to poor customer perception of the producer and potential loss of market share.

Test procedures can prevent the latter two situations from arising but extensive testing would incur additional costs.

The Japanese approach to quality is an all-pervasive one in which the quality of the product is seen as a consequence of the 'total quality' of the firm and its operations. The evolution of this concept has been outlined by Kobayashi (1986), chairman of NEC. Four stages in achieving total quality are described. Initially, in the 1960s, quality was seen by NEC as an issue of minimising the statistical dispersion of product performance from a standard value. By identifying the causes of non-conformance and treating this problem at source, the dispersion would narrow. Thus, if the inputs into the process are correctly balanced and fault-free, the product itself should be of high quality.

This was further developed in a second stage by the introduction of feedback loops, in Kobayashi's words, by 'considering a company as an amplifying circuit, and obtaining stable and distortion-free output' by applying customers' feedback to the circuit (1986, p. 6). For example, the sales department would feed back dissatisfaction to the relevant department; research, design, manufacturing, personnel and so on. Small group activities, or quality circles, were introduced into NEC at this time in order to involve all employees in the feedback process.

The third stage was the 'zero defects' programme which developed from NEC's observations of US defence equipment manufacture. The aim was to eliminate errors entirely through the stimulation of the quality groups. This concept spread quickly through Japanese industry, particularly via relations between component suppliers and product assemblers – zero-defect assembly requires zero-defect components. It was this emphasis on component quality which began to change in firms' relations with their suppliers – from simple, market transactions to more formal and long-term relationships.

Most recently, as a consequence of recession in the world economy, in the

1970s the 'total quality' concept was developed. Kobayashi identifies seven elements to quality:

- management;
- products and service;
- individual behaviour;
- working life;
- relationships with regional communities;
- corporate performance; and
- corporate image.

The last item – 'quality of corporate image' – is a consequence of the others and is synonymous with excellence in reputation. Products are sold on the basis of the identification with a company that is 'excellent' in all its actions and outputs. The decision of the customer to buy is presumed to be based not simply upon low prices or guarantees. Instead, it appears that the objective is to create a sense of trust that the product or service will be better or more reliable than its rivals. The company's reputation will depend upon that trust remaining intact.

Of course if the company is to achieve total quality, its suppliers must be similarly driven, or it must find ways of imposing adequate discipline on their inputs into its processes.

The extent to which TSE firms are able to exercise influence or control over their suppliers may be determined principally by the extent of internalisation or integration. Suppliers may be *external* – existing as a separate business – or they may be *internal*, for example a semiconductor division of a telecommunications firm. Firms face a choice between externalised or internalised sources of supply of components. In addition, component suppliers may or may not be integrated with TSE firms. The degree of integration of supply is – in theory at least – a matter of strategic choice for TSE firms. Figure 2.1 illustrates the four general relationships that may exist between TSE firms and component suppliers.

Which quadrant in Figure 2.1 represents the 'best' relationship between a TSE firm and its suppliers will vary between circumstances. It will also be contingent on national and corporate factors, as well as the technical characteristics of the components and their use in products. In each case, different sets of costs and benefits must be weighed. For example, a firm which relies heavily on custom components in its product design will face a different choice to one that makes use of industry-standard components. Lead times for custom component designs in relation to the length of product life cycles may have a significant bearing on the optimal choice of supplier relationship. It may be that rapid changes of product design and manufacturing technique will directly affect the degree of commitment that the TSE firm will be able to give to an individual supplier: there may be a trade-off between scale economies, procurement flexibility and security or reliability of

---

INTEGRATED FIRMS

| TSE firm's design/production
by licensed supplier | In-house design and production by
TSE firm's semiconductor division |

EXTERNALISED   INTERNALISED

SUPPLY   SUPPLY

| Industry standard design/production
by non-TSE firms | Industry standard design/production
by TSE firm's semiconductor
subsidiary |

NON-INTEGRATED FIRMS

Figure 2.1 Relationships between TSE firms and component supplies (Example: supply of integrated-circuit components)

supply. Indeed the organisation or phasing of supply for the production process is of major significance for costs and flexibility. For example, a firm may be able to engage in large-scale production yet retain output flexibility by the use of 'just-in-time' (JIT) methods without the overhead costs incurred by large inventories of components.

The management of manufacturing

Determining the effectiveness of all the elements of manufacturing competitiveness is managerial capability and 'operations strategy'. The Policy Studies Institute (1986) presents evidence that excellence in Japanese manufacturing derives from management techniques as much as from the design and physical characteristics of production facilities. The management of labour and the introduction of new technology; relations with suppliers; quality control; and linking product design with other aspects of manufacturing all require operational management to be optimally carried out. The quality of communications and information flows within the firm are particularly important in this regard. Flexibility and increased complexity are a consequence of advanced manufacturing capability. Management's ability to cope with this is a key determinant of successful implementation of integrated manufacturing strategies.

The following case study by Naegele (1987) illustrates this point. The combination of automation, JIT and low-defect manufacturing has been taken up as a major strategy by Northern Telecom in the manufacture of line cards at Raleigh, North Carolina (Naegele, 1987). Competitive pressure required low-cost, high-volume production which necessitated a switch from a batch process to a real-time process-control system. Continuous monitoring of the manufacturing process – associated with the extensive automation – replaced sample testing, reduced labour costs and enabled a yield of 99.2 per cent of acceptable quality products. The quality of incoming components must therefore be appropriately high and the role of component testing has been pushed down to suppliers. Only 25 per cent of components are now tested, so further savings are achieved both in eliminating this function and through the consequent JIT and low-inventory requirements. Product design is important to the process. In order to ensure the manufacturing system works effectively, design control is shared with the production engineers. This influence pervades the CAD software used by the product-development team, to ensure 'design for manufacture' of the firm's products.

Issues for empirical investigation

The international TSE industry operates in a rapidly changing technological and competitive environment. The success and, indeed, survival of TSE firms is necessarily determined by the relationship between technological change and competitiveness, as well as external factors such as regulatory change. In view of the preceding discussion of economies of scale and scope, and the role of manufacturing, it is clear that economic theory alone can offer little guidance to the future development of the TSE industry or to the problems and opportunities facing firms within it. Empirical investigation is required if the complex relationship between technological change and competitiveness is to be properly understood.

As a preface to the present empirical study of the TSE industry, the main issues for investigation are summarised below. This list of questions arises from a pragmatic interpretation of scale and scope economies and the nature of manufacturing in high-technology industry.

- To what extent do TSE firms compete directly with each other? Do they engage in strategies aimed at reducing competitive confrontation – such as geographical or product zoning – either consciously or for historical or structural reasons?
- What are the main aspects of competition between TSE firms – costs, price, product quality, technical superiority?
- What are the main factors determining the 'competitiveness' – ie the ability to compete and degree of success in competition – of TSE firms?
- What is the relationship between product and process technologies in TSE production? Does the same relationship apply to *all* firms, including those of comparable size?
- To what extent does the size of TSE firms (ie their potential for scale economies) determine their ability to compete with rivals? What are the main sources of scale economies in TSE production – manufacturing, component sourcing, R & D, marketing? Is there a minimum viable scale of activity in TSE production, either within market segments or overall?

- To what extent does the variety in the range of outputs of TSE firms (ie their potential for scope economies) determine their ability to compete with rivals? What are the main sources of scope economies in TSE production? Is there a minimum viable range of outputs for TSE firms?
- How does the organisation of manufacturing at divisional level affect the production capabilities of TSE firms?
- Do TSE firms consider there to be a best-practice technology for manufacturing and for production activities? If so, what is it?
- What (if any) barriers to market entry and exit exist in the TSE industry?
- What are the likely future implications for TSE firms of current relationships between technological change and competitiveness?

Appendix to Chapter 2

Manufacturing in TSE

As this study is based on empirical evidence from a particular industry – telecommunications subscriber equipment – the issues arising within the manufacturing sphere of the firm are different in detail from those of other sectors. Although broad thematic points can be made they are generalisations of specific problems or opportunities within a specialised production process. It is therefore appropriate to include a brief overview of this process which explains some of the specific technical issues.

The fundamental elements of a TSE product are, firstly, printed circuit boards (PCB) mounted with semiconductor devices and secondly, discrete components. These make up most of the hardware value of the product. They are mounted within a casing, connected with wires and interface connectors and in most cases they are provided with a power supply. The manufacturing process is essentially that of populating the PCBs with components then assembling the complete units, with several stages of testing and validation. (Figure 2.2 provides a simple description of telephone manufacture.)

Within a terminal device, such as a telephone, the plastics assembly takes up a more significant part of the process, the free movement of keys and buttons being vital for customer acceptability. The acoustic elements in the handset may be part of the assembly process although some firms buy the integrated capsules as components.

TSE firms may also engage in various forms of component manufacture either on-site or within different plants or divisions. This may include the PCBs, discrete or integrated components, wiring, plastic mouldings, other casings, power units and, in broader terminal types, cathode-ray tubes, liquid-crystal displays, and xerographic components for facsimile equipment.

The main element of the production process is the assembly of the circuits. The printed circuit board is 'an insulating substrate with conducting tracks

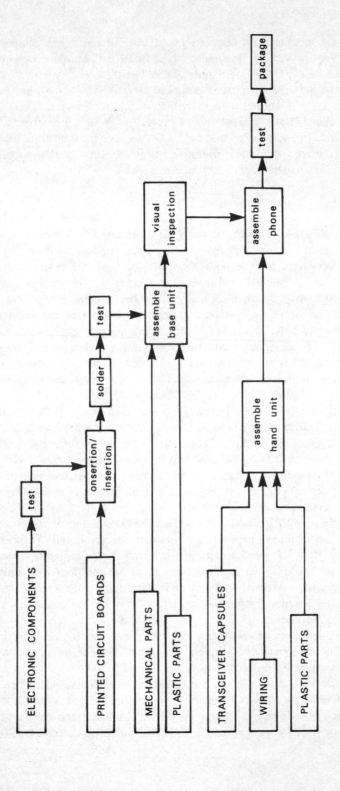

Figure 2.2 Outline of telephone-manufacturing process

onto which are mounted and connected a number of electronic components'
(O'Reilly, 1986, p. 11). In the simplest type of PCB the circuit may involve
tracks on one side of the board only (such boards are commonly used in
telephones). In the case of a more complex product, PCBs may have many
layers of tracks in a sandwich form with connections between layers being
made via 'plated holes'. The manufacture of these bare boards is a
customised and, in the case of multilayer boards, complex process. For this
reason, it is often performed in-house, although this is not necessarily
required as many independent manufacturers exist.

Assembly

The components are mounted onto the PCB using one of two main methods,
insertion or surface mount (onsertion). The usual method until recently has
been insertion, where the component's leads (or legs) are inserted through
holes in the board, 'clinched' and trimmed to secure. These are then soldered
on the underside to establish electrical contact between the component leads
and the tracks of the PCB. This process may be undertaken manually, semi-
automatically or totally automatically depending on the level of investment
and suitability of components for machine insertion. Insertion speeds run
from 200 per hour for manual assembly up to 6,000 per hour maximum for
fully automatic insertion, although actual rates will lie between these two
figures (O'Reilly, 1986).

The newer form of mounting is surface mount assembly (SMA) whereby
the devices are placed on to conducting pads on the surface of the PCB, fixed
with adhesive, then soldered in position, often using different soldering
techniques from insertion. Several advantages accrue from SMA: the
components are smaller and can be more densely packed; the lack of leads
means both sides of a board can be used; and placement is much easier and
quicker than insertion, so mounting speeds can be higher. If several placement heads are used then speeds of 5,000 to 15,000 components per hour can
be achieved, up to three times that of automatic insertion and 70 times that
of manual insertion. However, there are currently some difficulties with the
introduction of SMA. Three particular problems are the poor availability of
certain components, the difficulty of handling bare chip components so
making manual assembly impossible and the nature of the soldering techniques which make rework of faulty boards difficult.

After insertion/onsertion (both may be used sometimes to allow for use of
non-surface mount components) the components need to be soldered either by
wave soldering, where the board passes over a wave of molten solder, or reflow
soldering, where the solder is on the board in paste form and is heated to
'reflow' and establish contact. Generally the former method is used for one-
sided insertion boards and the latter for SMA. Some surface mount devices
(SMDs) can be fixed by wave soldering if they lie on the underside of the board.

The assembled circuit board will then be tested, sometimes after a period of 'soak' or 'burn in' to aid the weeding out of potential failures. Testing, also, is increasingly automated. In TSE – due to the need for 100 per cent reliability – it is typically of almost as much significance in terms of capital and labour costs as the assembly process.

Testing of sub-assemblies, especially complex and expensive boards for PABX, has two functions. Firstly, the test must separate good from bad sub-assemblies on the assumption that the cost of doing this is less than the later cost of repairing faulty final products or losing custom due to a reputation for faulty goods. Secondly, if the cost of the sub-assembly is sufficiently high, the fault must be diagnosed for repair and re-test. In some cases the cost of diagnostic testing and repair may be more than the value of the board in which case all failures are scrapped. However this latter case rarely applies in telecommunications, even to simple telephone boards, as the components are a high proportion of costs.

Testing may include visual inspection for obvious damage to the circuit tracks or wrongly fitted components. The board may then be placed in a test jig where probes subject it to an in-circuit test, automatically detecting faults. Functional tests may also be carried out in which the board is subjected to conditions similar to that of normal operation. Diagnosis is, however, usually more difficult in this latter case.

3 Market Structure and Commercial Developments in the TSE Industry

Segmenting the industry

Subscriber equipment forms the most open competitive sector of the telecommunications industry, yet that industry remains segmented and partially regulated. Within TSE, the most openly competitive product area is generally that of terminal equipment: telephones, facsimiles and the date-processing products capable of being connected to telecommunications networks. However, this product area is only relatively open; even in the case of the simple domestic telephone there are national distortions and differences in market openness and penetration.

In the past, regulatory structures have led to highly concentrated national telecommunications equipment markets, with four firm concentration ratios in the major producer countries in the late 1970s being of the order of 80 per cent (OECD, 1983). However, a considerable portion of this total revenue derives from the switching and transmission areas, whereas in TSE products there has always been a dualistic structure. In most countries major integrated manufacturers supply TSE and other telecommunications products in competition with a number of specialist niche TSE producers. TSE is also a sector in which the PTTs have often played a major role in development, marketing or even product manufacture as compared with a more simple procurement/

development assistance relationship with suppliers for network equipment.

TSE has been characterised in recent years by increased product segmentation as existing products – particularly telephones and PABX – have become increasingly differentiated by both price and non-price characteristics. The range of functions or features incorporated into products, and the aesthetic styling of household and office commodity products, have both developed rapidly. In addition a number of new products have emerged mainly concerned with data transfer and networking, with the prospects of wider use of video-based products in the future (teleconferencing, videotex, cable TV).

Current moves towards standardisation of transmission networks have not yet, however, had much impact on the range of TSE products. A number of new transmission networks have been developed in recent years, especially related to data transfer. These have helped expand the market for digital-data-transmission equipment networks (as opposed to modems) but their convergence into Integrated Services Digital Networks (ISDN) will still allow a multitude of new types of terminal equipment. Indeed as ISDN provides a standard network through which a PABX can transmit digital signals from a wide variety of sources with different interfaces, it provides an opportunity for further product specialisation and segmentation.

Regulatory change and markets

The regulatory situation in the major telecommunications markets is highly complex and changing. There is a continued evolution of liberalisation, dismantling of monopoly and changes in status of both service providers and manufacturers. Clearly, the relationship between the regulatory structure of service provision and the control over procurement is vital to the market situation and the potential for competitive behaviour in the equipment supply industry. Yet the literature on liberalisation, in the main, concentrates on the supply of services, the entry of new networks and service providers and the impacts on tariffs (see for example Tunstall, 1986). Only in a few cases do the studies examine the network–manufacturer complex, in a way that can be compared with the better-known defence industry complex. It is therefore the intention here to draw upon information about regulatory change and its impact on competition in equipment supply to explain the environment in which TSE firms must operate.

Regulatory policy is not the only area in which national governments can have an impact on TSE manufacturers. Financial and fiscal support for firms in electronics-based sectors is widespread, especially for new product development, new manufacturing processes, component development and for facilities in depressed or underdeveloped regions. Government also plays a role in the restructuring of industry, either intervening directly to bring about mergers or indirectly to restrict merger or monopoly through competition policy. Specific references to such non-regulatory policies will be restricted to the role of governments, in changing the structure of the industry participants and in new technological developments.

The regulatory situation within a specific country can be regarded as either *market regulation*, in which the PTT or major carrier is in a government-regulated position with suppliers being subject to some restriction, or *competitive regulation* (Willats, 1982). This second option is the liberalised or 'open' market in which government intervention is aimed at maintaining competition and increasing the role of market forces in equipment or service provision.

The general tendency worldwide has been for a shift away from market regulation towards competitive regulation. This has been particularly prevalent in the supply of subscriber equipment, where the monopoly of the service carrier over the distribution or even the ownership of equipment has been dismantled. Such liberalisation is frequently partial or phased in, so that in many countries some TSE products are supplied on an open basis whereas others, usually the primary domestic telephone, are under monopoly control. A second caveat in liberalised markets is that 'open' competition may be limited to firms satisfying particular criteria. All countries impose technical standards on equipment to ensure compatability with the network, but additionally some countries may use standards to exclude non-domestic suppliers. Type approval may be used by the national government or the major carrier to delay the market entry of foreign firms, to offer temporary protection to domestic suppliers, or indeed to prohibit the sale of imported equipment completely.

Europe

Within the European Community, liberalisation has increased dramatically in recent years after the pace-setting of the UK and with the prospect of the Single European Market in 1992. The European Commission has targeted telecommunications as a key sector where the benefits of new products and services, and of the creation of a European scale market are hindered by national regulatory barriers. It has therefore developed a number of policy approaches including that of negotiating liberalisation in the supply of subscriber equipment and that of standardising network interfaces to allow for the interoperability of networks, terminals and services.

Figure 3.1 shows the extent to which private competition has been introduced into the supply of TSE. This may have been either as a consequence of breaking the monopoly of the PTT, or allowing new products to be sold in a competitive situation from the beginning. The fundamental issue is the supply of the first telephone which is still restricted to the monopoly network operator in all but France and the UK. As terminal equipment moves further towards data processing equipment and new services (modems,

68

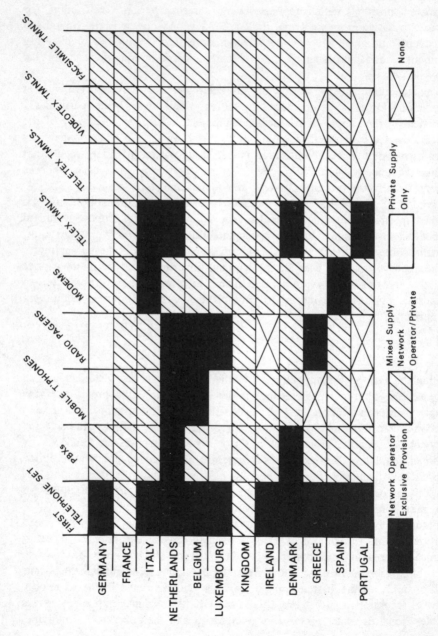

Figure 3.1 Survey of European terminal equipment regulatory supply conditions April 1987

teletex, videotex, cellular phones), the more liberalised is the supply. In many cases no monopoly has ever been established.

Two important papers from the European Commission set out the future development of telecommunications liberalisation in Europe. The first, *Towards a Dynamic European Economy: Green Paper on the Development of the Common Market for Telecommunications Services and Equipment* was published in 1987. This clearly states the intention of the European Commission to take the initiative in the liberalisation process in Europe so as to allow for the free movement of equipment and to eliminate restrictions on service provision: to establish a 'level playing field' (Narjes, 1988). The Green Paper reviews the current situation and sets out the basic objectives of the Commission arising out of the need to achieve the Single Market – primary objective of the EC established by the Single European Act of 1987.

In early 1988 this was followed by a paper outlining the proposals for implementing the Green Paper, and reporting on the current state of negotiations towards the Single Market (CEC, 1988). Two elements are of significance for TSE. Firstly, the supply of terminals (including all TSE products) is to be fully liberalised by 1991. By this time all private and domestic subscribers will be able to buy equipment on the open market subject to type approval. Telecommunications administrations will be able to sell or lease equipment in competition with private firms.

Secondly, the standardisation of networks and interfaces will be undertaken by a European institute for telecommunications standards. This will speed up the process of standardisation, without which national differentiation will persist, so that a genuine Single Market is created, rather than a collection of 12 national markets, each with a similar degree of openness.

As a consequence of these moves, the Netherlands has announced complete liberalisation of terminal equipment beginning from January 1989. However, the biggest change in Europe is likely to be in the West German market for telephones, the biggest remaining monopolised market by value. Other smaller countries retain a more complete monopoly than the West Germans but are less attractive in economic terms without standardisation with other countries. Overall market size in these smaller markets, such as Belgium, is equal only to that of a regional market in France, the UK or FRG.

United Kingdom

Prior to 1981 the UK telecommunications service was a government monopoly within the PTT, the General Post Office (GPO). Telecommunications equipment was supplied by private domestic companies, to the PTT for distribution. However, the GPO effectively controlled the product-development process for all but a few products through its research laboratories and monopolistic procurement. Only PABX of over 100 lines were exempt from the monopoly and indeed the Post Office was excluded from that market. In this restrictive environment the domestic manufacturers had established a close relationship with a PTT which had been slow to introduce electronic technology into its network. Consequently, even in the private market for PABX, the UK manufacturers were relatively uncompetitive offering older electromechanical designs as opposed to electronic products from IBM, Ericsson and ITT (Hills, 1986).

By 1979 there were a number of pressures on the Post Office and the government to modernise the network, provide new services (especially in the City of London), open up supply of equipment and remove telecommunications investment from the public sector borrowing requirement. The Telecommunication Bill was introduced in 1980 to establish British Telecom as a distinct entity – separate from postal services – in a more liberalised market. Thus BT would lose its monopoly over all but the supply of the first telephone instrument and control over technical standards would be removed to an independent body. However BT would continue to compete in the supply of all TSE products but would have to do so through arms-length subsidiaries without cross-subsidisation.

One contentious point was that BT should be allowed to retain its monopoly of PABX maintenance. The manufacturers regarded this as both over-optimistic given the range of PABX that BT would need to be competent to maintain, and potentially threatening in that BT would need a software competence for the new digital equipment that could be used to introduce centrex services into the public network. This point was therefore amended to refer only to analogue equipment.

Despite liberalisation, new products were slow to arrive and the Department of Trade and Industry (DTI) soon had to intervene, certifying all existing telephones used by BT for private supply and inviting applications from manufacturers. Yet of 96 submitted telephone designs only one was of UK origin. The UK firms appeared to be reluctant to compete with BT, partly due to a lack of marketing and sales organisation and experience, but also due to a perception of the danger of openly competing with their largest customer. BT responded by announcing it would set up a retail business to sell telephones, including those of the UK firms, as well as foreign imports and, significantly, BT-manufactured telephones from its former refurbishment factory in South Wales. Still, by 1982, only one new telephone and no PABX had been approved for connection. Despite the involvement of DTI, BT was still testing equipment and posing technical problems for firms seeking approval for their products.

With the sale of BT shares, and the corporation's effective removal from government control, the remaining monopoly over the primary instrument was removed. The UK manufacturers had attempted to limit BT's market share of telephone supply to 25 per cent by regulation, but this option was not adopted. BT was allowed to continue both manufacturing and supplying telephones, and it retained dominance with an 82 per cent share in the supply market in 1985.

A number of consequences of this liberalisation have emerged which are of some importance for this study. Whilst BT's share of the UK market has only fallen slightly, the UK manufacturers have been the main losers. BT has sourced more products from overseas, and imports have also gained a substantial share of independent sales, particularly telephones sold through high street retailers and mail order firms. Imports have risen rapidly from 8 per cent in 1981 to 17 per cent in 1985, and the total number of suppliers in the UK market has increased. Thus by 1986 some 28 firms had gained approval for 90 new simple telephones with an additional 29 complex telephones from 14 suppliers (MMC, 1986a, 1986b).

In the PABX market BT was allowed monopoly status for longer than for the supply of second telephones. This period was used to boost the replacement rate of small PABX, with 70 per cent being replaced between 1981–6, 90 per cent of them by BT. In addition to dominating the supply and maintenance of PABX, BT also acquired a controlling stake in Mitel – an ailing Canadian PABX firm – despite the reservations of the Monopolies and Mergers Commission. The Department of Trade and Industry overruled the MMC's views. However the close relationship between BT, GEC and Plessey – arising out of years of collaboration – led to the two main UK suppliers retaining 59 per cent of the UK market in 1984–5 with higher shares still of the larger size exchanges where Plessey's ISDN has been particularly successful.

Despite the opening up of the UK market, the ability of BT to exert market dominance has for the moment helped retain a substantial market share for UK manufacturers, and indeed has given an opportunity for other UK electronics firms to enter telecommunications, specifically Ferranti, Racal and Thorn EMI (all with overseas collaboration). Other consequences have been that price competition has increased, firms have had to develop marketing capabilities, and the long-established technical collaboration between BT and its suppliers has virtually ended. The extent of liberalisation has also led to increased inward investment from Japanese, North American and European manufacturers. It is possible that the activities of such firms may lead to further changes in the ownership structure of the UK industry in the future.

Federal Republic of Germany

The West German market of telecommunications products is generally acknowledged to be one of the most protective in Europe, although in reality only the primary telephone is subject to the monopoly of the Deutsche Bundepost (DBp) (see Figure 3.1). Nevertheless, it is one of the largest markets available to European manufacturers. Prices have been maintained at high levels by virtue of low levels of foreign penetration and a reluctance by domestic manufacturers to engage in a price war.

The DBp is constituted as an organ of the state under the direction of the minister for posts and telecommunications and an administrative council. This council includes representatives of the federal and state governments, employees of the DBp (who are also members of the post office workers union), industry representatives and a technical expert who is usually from Siemens (Morgan and Webber, 1986).

The DBp only provides services. It has no manufacturing functions although it is active in the supply of certain equipment for rental or purchase in competition with private suppliers. The only monopoly of supply is for the leasing of the first telephone set at the main station. The DBp does not supply mobile phones, pagers, telex terminals or teletex terminals leaving these purely to private suppliers.

Despite liberalisation of the supply of equipment, the DBp has total control over the establishment of technical standards for privately supplied TSE through its telecommunications engineering centre (FTZ). Type approval is then undertaken by the 'central approval office for telecommunications' (ZZF) which reports directly to the ministry for posts and telecommunications.

The links between the DBp and the German manufacturers are close and institutionalised. In technical matters there are a number of firms to which the DBp predictably turns for support. For the smaller firms in particular which may be niche suppliers of telephones for example, the relationship with the DBp and indeed the larger firms is one of dependent sub-contractor, and these small firms would be particularly vulnerable to liberalisation. Their ability to lobby on technical committees, supported by the unions, politicians and industry associations, that liberalisation will lead to job loss is an effective tool preventing change.

The larger firms are in a favourable position also, to supply at higher prices than elsewhere and become closely involved in standards setting. Given that industry in the Federal Republic faces high labour costs these issues are important, even for the largest firms such as Siemens.

Pressure has been mounting against this close-knit structure from two sources. Firstly, it has come from firms within Germany which have had difficulties in gaining access to the market, including Nixdorf and IBM, who have criticised the use of high standards and restrictive procurement policies. Secondly, there is pressure on the DBp from outside Germany as a consequence of the integration of European markets. Such national restrictive practices are consequently to be withdrawn before 1992. It is unclear as yet how this will develop, but other European manufacturers, for example from France and the UK, are attracted to a large and relatively highly priced market, and will be lobbying vigorously for full liberalisation by 1992.

France

The recent history of telecommunications in France has been notable for two major phases of development: massive investment in a digital network in the late 1970s and corporate reorganisation in the 1980s. Prior to the major public investment programme of the 1970s, France had an extremely low telephone density with very poor infrastructure. In response to this '*crise du telephone*', the Direction Generale des Telecommunications (DGT) instituted a massive renewal programme, installing new digital exchanges to leapfrog into a world-leading technical position (investment 1976–80 of 120 bn francs).

The DGT became the key factor within a strong national planning framework for the development of 'telematics'. A strategy to spread the active use of telecommunications throughout French society – and so gain an international comparative advantage – was developed under the 'plan telematique' of 1978. However the supply-led approach to stimulating adoption of advanced services and terminals met with problems that had been absent in the earlier network modernisation. The paternal authoritarianism of the introduction of new terminals, and the lack of clarity and coordination in the development of the technology and service elements led to considerable unease (Morgan and Webber, 1986).

From 1981 under Mitterand the role of the state grew through the nationalisation and restructuring of much of the production sector, and the granting to DGT responsibility for the '*Plan Filiere Electronique*'. Despite this the DGT under new leadership backed away from telematics into a new round of network modernisation. More recently there has been denationalisation of CGCT, CGE Alcatel and Matra.

The French telecommunication authority is a directorate of the PTT, the ministry for posts and telecommunications. Formerly known as the Direction Generale des Telecommunications (DGT) and recently renamed France Telecom it is subject to regulation by parliament, presidential decree and councils of state. In addition, part of this responsibility has, since 1987, been transferred to a new organisation, the Commission Nationale de la Communication et des Libertes (CNCL).

France Telecom is responsible for network provision, under a general monopoly of infrastructure and basic services, and supplies terminal equipment and advanced services on a liberalised basis. No new network providers have been licensed, with the exception of some private or closed networks, and a new cellular network announced in 1988.

The existing telephone network is the most highly digitalised in the world as a consequence of the country's major investments in the 1970s. This has also supported the growth of the largest videotex service, with over 3.4 million minitel terminals installed (around 14 per cent of total subscribers). The rapid growth of new terminals, the replacement of rotary dial telephones and the expansion and enhancement of the networks have all contributed to a buoyant market for TSE products.

All terminal equipment supply has now been liberalised, with the disbandment of the monopoly of the primary telephone in 1986. France Telecom has no manufacturing facilities so its role is limited to distribution and rental in competition with manufacturers and private distributors. Large PABXs are an exception in that France Telecom opted out of the market for supply or rental, leaving this market segment to the manufacturers who have greater expertise in installation and maintenance.

Future liberalisation in France is expected to concentrate on advanced services such as Value Added Network Services (VANS), cable and cellular communications (Roulet, 1988). The benefits of rapid growth in services as a consequence of this would be a further aid to the development of the terminal market. The success of the videotex experiment, for example, would indicate that advanced cable services may generate a substantial market for such equipment. In cellular telephony, growth up to the present has been limited, compared with the UK, but the licensing of a second consortium network may stimulate growth. The new operator will be a partnership between Compagnie Generale des Eaux (a water distribution group), Alcatel and Nokia of Finland. Nokia, it should be noted, has also a joint venture with Matra for the manufacture of cellular phones; Matra being France Telecom's partner in the existing Radiocom 2000 cellular network.

Sweden

A different industrial structure has developed in Sweden where the telecommunications agency, Televerket, is a public service corporation operating in a commercial environment. It has no formal monopoly and it is under relatively loose control by the small ministry of transport and communications. Indeed Richardson (1986) claims that within the ministry only two or three people deal with telecommunications policy matters out of a staff of 85. Televerket, however, is one of the most complex integrated-service providers in the world. It provides telephony, telex, teletex, videotex, mobile telephony, digital radio paging and data-communications networks. It also distributes radio and TV and is involved in manufacturing, R & D and distribution of telecommunication products. Unlike other European network operators its remit has never included postal services.

Fundamental to the structure of the Swedish telecommunications industry is the relationship between Televerket and Ericsson particularly through a joint development company, Ellemtel Utvecklings AB. This collaboration has led to the development of the AXE switching system and some TSE products. These are manufactured by Televerket's subsidiary, Teli, for Swedish consumption and by Ericsson for external markets. Teli supplies a high proportion of its output to Televerket. This was formerly 95 per cent (Richardson, 1986) but is now falling as Teli seeks overseas sales through new sales offices in the UK and USA. By 1986 89 per cent of output was still going to Televerket (Teli, 1986).

The Swedish market is relatively open, with monopoly supply by Televerket being limited (since 1985) to PABX, high-speed modems and public payphones. Televerket's internal production capability enables it to be a very effective purchaser, and it is prepared to source from overseas if it is unhappy with the offerings from Ericsson. Some 15 to 20 per cent of Televerket's telecommunications purchasing is from foreign manufacturers. Richardson (1986) suggests that Ericsson has perhaps benefited from this discipline and from the liberal trade policy which has allowed the firm to source overseas if necessary. The fact that Teli supplies the bulk of the core local market has meant that Ericsson must concentrate on export and overseas production. However, part of Ericsson's product development costs are covered by Televerket – Teli's parent company.

Televerket is subject to government pressures for open competitive procurement. Liberalisation of Televerket's monopoly continues on an evolving basis partly in response to technological developments and the maintenance of a very sophisticated telecommunications market. Type approval, for example, no longer requires testing within Televerket's laboratories but can be tested elsewhere according to Televerket's technical requirements. This was partly a response to the emergence of 'private' telephone sets not conforming to Swedish standards, which made up to 10 per cent of new telephones at one point. A liberal approval regime allowed Televerket to reimpose technical standards for telephones, to resolve problems in the operation of the network caused by non-standard products (Richardson, 1986).

The Swedish market is marked by a high level of technical sophistication. It has a national digital network, the highest telephone density in the world, and a high degree of penetration of other new products and services such as computer terminals, cellular telephony, digital PABX, videotex and other data transmission. The combination of this and close collaboration with other Nordic countries and the EC is likely to be a great benefit to the Swedish manufacturers as they seek export markets, although the potential for new competition between the two major firms may prove problematic.

United States

The regulatory environment in the USA is both liberal and extremely complex. The absence of a state monopoly PTT prior to liberalisation ensured a complex framework of network providers, manufacturers and regulation. Since liberalisation the market structures in networks and equipment have both become more complex, and several phases of legislation have affected the boundaries within which firms may operate.

Prior to 1984 the bulk of US telecommunications activity lay within the integrated AT & T monopoly. This included the majority of the public network, and the manufacturing of much of the installed equipment. AT & T had a monopoly over the supply of TSE to its network subscribers. The *de facto* monopoly position led to a number of anti-trust suits by the US Department of Justice, culminating in the 1982 judgement by Judge Greene breaking up the company.

The Modification of Final Judgement (MFJ) by Judge Green aimed to prevent AT & T from abusing its control over the local network in order to keep out long distance carrier and equipment manufacturing rivals. The removal of this network from AT & T's control would therefore allow equal access to the subscriber for all long-distance carriers and TSE suppliers, also preventing AT & T from cross-subsidisation to manipulate prices. The local area networks were grouped into seven independent Regional Bell Operating Companies (RBOCs), with AT & T keeping its long lines, international services, R & D and manufacturing.

Under this new arrangement the RBOCs would still be able to supply subscriber equipment, but would not be allowed to manufacture equipment. The RBOCs were also required to avoid discrimination between AT & T and other suppliers of goods and services. This included equipment procurement as well as access to inter-exchange carrier networks. More recently a new review by Judge Greene relaxed some restrictions on the RBOCs by allowing them to offer data-transmission services (but not supply information for VADS). However, the restrictions on manufacturing were unaffected. The RBOCs disclaimed any intention of becoming major telecommunications manufacturers but wanted the ability to enter collaborations with those suppliers requiring development capability or niche product manufacturing. The capability was firmly refused.

The Federal Communications Commission had over a number of years sought to liberate the supply and connection of TSE to the network. For example the FCC instituted a registration procedure for third-party equipment suppliers to connect equipment to the network. This created a market for interconnect equipment vendors. In 1980 this was strengthened by the FCC's second computer inquiry decision which required AT & T to itemise TSE rental charges separately from service charges, and to offer new terminal equipment through a separate subsidiary. The FCC controls the registration of terminals, setting technical standards in consultation with carriers, manufacturers and users.

The effect of these moves was to shift the balance from rented to private ownership in the space of one year. In 1983 70 per cent of telephones were leased, in 1984 the market was 60 per cent private ownership (OECD, 1987). Consequently the equipment market in the US has become extremely competitive. For example Western Electric's (AT & T) share of the PBX market fell from 60–80 per cent in 1973 to 19.1 per cent in 1983. Prices of simple telephones are said to be as low as three or four dollars in New York (Baughcum, 1986).

The TSE market structure has therefore become considerably more complex than before. The RBOCs still retain a major role in supplying TSE to subscribers although these may be sourced from any manufacturer. Consequently many overseas firms are gaining entry to the US market via RBOCs, especially those firms that have established a strong presence via acquisition or inward investment. Firms also sell direct to the public and business via retailers, business equipment suppliers or internal sales organisation. AT & T and other network operators with manufacturing operations compete openly with overseas and non-integrated firms via these various distribution forms.

Japan

The dominant force in Japanese telecoms is the partly privatised Nippon Telegraph and Telephone (NTT), the main provider of domestic public telecommunications services. Other type-1 service providers offer limited networks, for example Japan Telecom Co based upon the Japan National Railways communications network, or international services (Kokusai Denshin Denwa) – monopoly, but with an option for competition in the future.

The existing carriers are licensed and regulated by the ministry of posts and telecommunications (MPT) which establishes financial and technological criteria for their operation. Prior to 1985 and the implementation of the Telecommunications Business Law, there had been considerable debate over the role of the ministry for international trade and industry (MTI) in telecommunications policy. MTI and Japanese industrial firms were concerned over the domination by NTT of enhanced services, and they argued that NTT should be confined to basic services. NTT however were prepared to give up their monopoly in return for continued ability to provide the more profitable enhanced services. (Ito, 1986).

Along with liberalisation of services, a new approvals institute, JATE, was designated in April 1985, issuing type approval for terminal equipment. The sale of TSE products is not restricted to NTT, and PABX particularly are mostly supplied by private companies direct to customers. Gradually sales of TSE are widening to encompass a wider range within Japan and overseas. However, in terms of market share, foreign manufacturers are still finding difficulties in selling standard equipment. Specialised niche products are to some extent an exception and several non-Japanese firms reported some sales of such products to customers in Japan.

Product markets

The broadening range of products within TSE, the rapidly changing regulatory situation, and general growth in demand for advanced telecommunication services have led to a spectrum of product market trends.

Three general product trends can be identified in TSE. Firstly, in the domestic context, the telephone is being commoditised, and it is facing transformation due to a convergence with other domestic electronic systems and equipment. Secondly, the demand for enhanced services and the shortening of product life cycles are generating a large replacement market for private systems in countries where penetration of telecommunications was already high. Thirdly, there is extremely rapid growth in demand for new types of terminal equipment, particularly in data transmission, and in extending the reach of telecommunications in time and space (pagers, mobile telephony, electronic mail, voice mail).

The telephone

The effects of liberalisation and cost reduction have commoditised the telephone, so transforming it into a consumer electronics product. The switch from monopoly rental to high-street retail sale in many countries has created an opportunity for price-based competition and for the rapid adoption of features such as memories, last-number redial, on-hook dialling and cordless operation. This competition based on price and feature differentiation is typical of the consumer electronics sector.

In the UK particularly, the strength of the multiple retail chains in consumer electronics such as audio and video products has been of major benefit to low-cost firms seeking to enter the UK market giving them wide distribution. The Japanese consumer electronics firms have had considerable market success as a consequence of being able to deal direct with a high proportion of total retail outlets through these firms. Korean and Taiwanese firms have also used the same entry points, but often operating under OEM deals with the retailer 'badge engineering' products such as TVs and hi-fis. The same retailers have been extremely keen to get into telephone sales, and undercut the prices of British Telecom's retail business. These have consequently turned to the Koreans and Taiwanese to supply telephones also, often on an OEM basis.

European manufacturers have responded to this development by aiming for the higher margin 'designer-phone' market, cashing in on a general increased awareness of good design, and a rejection by more affluent households of cheap standard products. Thus for example, STC is supplying a commissioned telephone to Habitat, Teli is advertising designer-named telephones in interior-design magazines, and most firms are supplying a range of modern and traditional telephones with a rapid turnover of styling. However, a new threat to this strategy has come from the Japanese manufacturers with dominant brand names in audio and video products such as Sony, Hitachi, Toshiba and National Panasonic (Matsushita).

Most of the major core markets for telephones are already relatively saturated; Sweden is the most extreme case with 8.3 million telephones for eight million people (Richardson 1986). However, a strengthening replacement market is emerging, as old dial telephones are replaced by press-button analogue and then all-digital telephones with added features. The 'second telephone' and 'cordless telephone' markets are growing rapidly, aided by a trend towards more frequent replacement in the future. Currently in the UK, high rental charges make purchase a very attractive option. Annual rentals are higher than the cost of the cheapest Taiwanese telephones, and up to around one-third of the price of the higher quality European telephones (which are equivalent to the rented instrument). In the USA the cheaper imported telephone has similarly become downgraded to an item received free with gift tokens from petrol stations.

Table 3.1 World telephone-market projections

	Units sold (in thousands)			
	1985	1986	1987	1990
Europe	18,000	18,000	19,500	24,000
France	4600	4200	4600	5500
UK	5300	5300	5500	6500
West Germany	3400	3600	3800	4500
Italy	3000	3000	3200	4500
USA	30,000	31,000	32,000	35,000
Rest of the world	17,000	18,000	18,500	23,000
World total	65,000	67,000	70,000	82,000

Source: Firms' estimates

The production levels for telephones reflect these market trends. Output growth is low in Europe, and high output is now occurring in some of the newly industrialising countries.

Since 1978, Japanese output of telephone sets has risen dramatically. In the period 1982–5 it more than doubled in both volume and growth. Value initially rose more rapidly than volume and then more slowly and it could be expected that value would continue to rise at a slower rate than unit output. None the less, data from the EIAJ indicates a shift in production value away from standard handsets to higher-value multifunction telephones and other non-standard products. Exports, however, have been declining steadily from a high point in 1984 to 1986 with around a 30 per cent fall in value terms in two years.

Taiwan shows continued substantial export performance. Despite a small local market, it now manufactures approximately 20 million telephone sets per annum, most of which are exported, particularly to the United States. This aggregate total includes output from a number of large manufacturers,

Table 3.2 Forecasts for telecommunication equipment sales in US$m

1987			1988		
1.	United States	24,313	1.	United States	27,131
2.	Russia	9800	2.	Russia	13,402
3.	Japan	7100	3.	Japan	8456
4.	West Germany	6100	4.	West Germany	7684
5.	France	4960	5.	Italy	6734
6.	Italy	4522	6.	France	6161
7.	United Kingdom	3450	7.	United Kingdom	4718
8.	Canada	1927	8.	Spain	3000
9.	China	1752	9.	Canada	2321
10.	Spain	1650	10.	India	2282
11.	South Korea	1494	11.	China	2050
12.	India	1462	12.	South Korea	1919
13.	Australia	1360	13.	Australia	1732
14.	Switzerland	1150	14.	South Africa	1511
15.	South Africa	1142	15.	Switzerland	1393
16.	Sweden	966	16.	Mexico	1307
17.	Mexico	946	17.	Sweden	1144
18.	Brazil	895	18.	Austria	1080
19.	Austria	805	19.	Brazil	1024
20.	Indonesia	704	20.	Taiwan	913
21.	Taiwan	658	21.	Indonesia	876
22.	Argentina	697	22.	Netherlands	787
23.	Saudi Arabia	611	23.	Argentina	772
24.	Hong Kong	609	24.	Saudi Arabia	770
25.	Netherlands	562	25.	Hong Kong	705
26.	Norway	518	26.	Norway	643
27.	East Germany	464	27.	East Germany	602
28.	Belgium	436	28.	Pakistan	540
29.	Venezuela	428	29.	Belgium	519
30.	Greece	339	30.	Greece	503
31.	Pakistan	328	31.	Venezuela	482
32.	Singapore	328	32.	Singapore	428
33.	Finland	314	33.	Turkey	403
34.	Denmark	295	34.	Denmark	370
35.	Turkey	294	35.	New Zealand	386
36.	New Zealand	257	36.	Finland	364
37.	Bangladesh	246	37.	Bangladesh	317
38.	Poland	231	38.	Poland	305
39.	Egypt	228	39.	Iraq	283
40.	Hungary	211	40.	Egypt	280
41.	Iraq	201	41.	Czechoslovakia	274
42.	Yugoslavia	188	42.	Hungary	252

(Based on *Financial Times*, 1987)

one of which claims annual production of five million telephones. This would make it one of the top three manufacturers in the world by volume, although mainly at the low-value end.

The Third World is likely to become a key market battleground in the future, initially for basic telephone equipment. China, India, Mexico, Brazil and Indonesia are in the current top 20 world markets for telecommunications equipment with huge growth potential. The International Telecommunications Union (ITU) has set a goal of achieving one telephone for every six people in Latin America by 2000, a total of an additional 85 million lines. The Institute for Development Studies at Sussex University predicts that by 2000 the Third World will account for 57 per cent of global telecommunications investments compared with 8 per cent currently (Miller, 1988). Whilst the telephone is the simplest product for Third World countries to gain entry to the telecommunications market, there are already subsidiaries of major US, Japanese and European firms in many of these countries. It is likely that such local production will allow these firms to gain dominance in these markets without risking protectionist stances on imports.

Switching products

There has been considerable product development in key systems and PABX during recent years. This market, particularly, is hampered by the complexities of the coexistence of different generations of product, by differing regulatory classification of products (as in FRG) and by variations in standards, interconnection and levels of integration. (For example there is variation in the willingness of manufacturers to market PABX switches as ISDN products.)

The market for the first-generation electronic PABX is saturated in most advanced economies. Rapid improvements in the sophistication of new digital and ISDN PABXs, together with shortened product life cycles, have increased the rate of obsolence and replacement. This growth in the volume of the market, however, is mitigated by price reductions. Growth rates by value therefore have been small compared with the computer industry for example.

The best growth prospects remain at the smaller end of the market with key systems for small offices, and increasingly the diffusion of this type of product into the domestic household market, especially larger houses.

Large corporate telecommunications networks represent the opposite extreme of the market. Here, a PABX may be essentially an ISDN central-office switch in private use although functionality, control and call costing will be sufficiently different to require a different kind of switch to the PTT. The increasing sophistication of IT-based communications networks in larger organisations is creating a demand for very flexible ISDN PABXs that can bring together a number of different networks and interfaces including analogue telecommunications and local area networks (LANs) for distributed data processing.

However, the relevance of ISDN products and services to smaller users' needs is not clear. The expression '*interfaces subscribers don't need*' is still held to be true even for medium-sized firms. Manufacturers need to build a market for such systems. These newer systems are cheaper per extension to manufacture than previous generations of products, and therefore more competitive. The customer may feel that the sophistication provided as standard now is greater than that required. It is however more expensive for a manufacturer to produce updated older exchanges or to design a distinct non-ISDN new switch in addition to the standard ISDN model. For the user, it is more economical to underuse the new switch than to buy an older model that better matches its demands. The problem for manufacturers is to convince customers of this economic argument in favour of investment in 'excess' switching capacity.

New terminal equipment

New terminal equipment has been the major growth element of the TSE sector in recent years as a consequence of the growth of new forms of network, and new methods of message transmission on the telephone network. New networks have included cellular telephony, paging, teletex, videotex and interactive cable. Rapid growth in such networks has provided a dynamic in the market for many types of terminal, often with high profit margins. A similar growth has occurred for data terminals for the public telephone network, such as facsimile machines.

Cellular telephony has been one of the fastest growing parts of the telecommunication industry in recent years. Previous forms of mobile radio had serious technical limitations which reduced their market potential. Uneconomic use of the radio spectrum reduced capacity and led to queueing; interference was considerable; calls were not secure; encryption was impractical and the range of features offered was extremely limited (Law, 1986). Cellular technology overcame these problems very effectively, and also led to other benefits. The use of UHF as opposed to VHF bands for example, combined with the small cell size, means power requirements are much reduced – a considerable benefit for portability. Also the shorter wavelength can penetrate buildings and tunnels much more effectively. Capacity and quality are much higher than with previous systems, and new switching technology allows very sophisticated features to be incorporated into the network.

Initially, the strongest markets for cellular telecommunications were in the USA and Scandanavia with introduction around 1980 and rapid growth in the number of subscribers. The USA is now estimated to have over a million subscribers, the largest single market in the world, but market penetration is

Table 3.3 Telecommunication acquisitions and mergers in the 1980s

Shareholder(s)	Subsidiary/Associate Firm	Date	Comments
IBM	Rolm	1984	100% acquisition
BT	Mitel	1985	57% holding
CGE	ITT Telecommunication div	1986	To form Alcatel
GEC/Plessey	GPT	1988	Merged telecoms division
Northern Telecom	STC	1988	25% holding
Fujitsu/GTE	Fujitsu GTE Business Systems	1987	Fujitsu took 80% stake in GTE subsidiary
Racal/Plessey	Orbitel	1987	Joint venture formed
Autophon	Comdial (European div.)	1985	Comdial divestment
ATT	Olivetti	n/a	25% stake
ATT/Philips	ATP	n/a	Joint venture
Matra/Ericcson	CGCT	1987	Joint acquisition
NCR	Ztel	n/a	19% investment in new PBX firm
Wang	Intecom	n/a	20% holding in PBX firm
Robert Bosch	Telenorma	1981	80% stake, raised in 1987 to 100%
Robert Bosch	Jeumont Schneider	1987	35% stake/increased

much higher in the Scandanavian countries. Figure 3.2 shows penetration rates in Norway and Sweden of the order of 29–35 per thousand population. Japan, another early adopter, has seen much lower uptake with only 59,000 subscribers by February 1986 and one estimate of 125,000 by the end of 1987 (*Financial Times*, 19.10.87). Future growth in Japan is, however, expected to be much more rapid with estimates of up to 4.5 million subscribers by 2000.

The UK has been the biggest growth market of the second-stage adopters with over 300,000 subscribers in mid-1988 after a start up in January 1985. This is around five times the size of any other EC national market, where growth rates have been inhibited perhaps by PTT monopoly. In the UK, active competition between BT Cellnet and Racal Vodaphone has stimulated awareness of the service, and open supply of equipment has led to relatively low prices. Consequently, high foreign penetration of the UK cellular TSE market has been achieved, but the existence of a large installed base has been an incentive for UK manufacturers to respond with new products, especially for the future pan-European digital service (PEDS).

Mintel estimate the six largest suppliers of cellular equipment in Europe in 1986 to be: Motorola, Philips, Thomson (Alcatel), Ericsson, Storno, Mobira

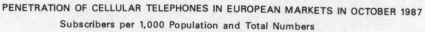

PENETRATION OF CELLULAR TELEPHONES IN EUROPEAN MARKETS IN OCTOBER 1987
Subscribers per 1,000 Population and Total Numbers

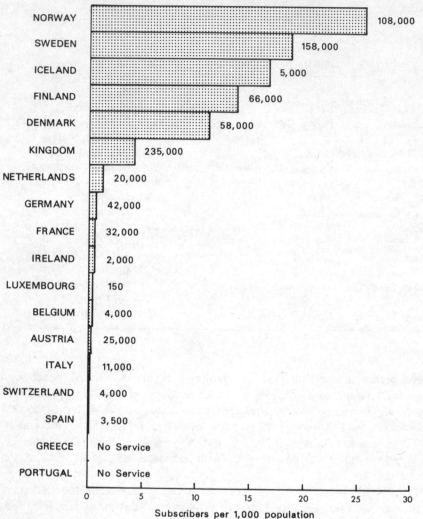

Figure 3.2   Penetration of cellular telephones in European markets in October 1987

(Nokia). The acquisition of Storno by Motorola has since given them considerable market leadership. The European markets vary somewhat in terms of leading players, with most being dominated by their domestic suppliers – West Germany by Bosch, AEG and Siemens for example. In open markets such as Scandanavia and the UK the range of suppliers is considerably greater. Japanese competition (NEC, Panasonic and Mitsubushi) is strong in the UK. In Sweden high adoption rates have led to Ericsson reaching agreements with Volvo and Saab to install equipment in cars as a standard option.

The US market is also highly competitive and fragmented with the lead suppliers being Motorola, Oki, General Electric, Panasonic, E.F. Johnson, Hitachi and Ericsson. Price cutting has been very keen, and Motorola filed a petition to the US Department of Commerce claiming that at least nine Japanese manufacturers were dumping products in the USA at only half the price of comparable units in Japan. In response, anti-dumping margins were imposed on the Japanese producers: up to 106.6 per cent in the case of Matsushita.

Although the car-bourne phone has been the main form of diffusion of cellular technology, the hand-portable version has become increasingly popular as higher levels of component integration have made this possible. In the UK one new firm – Technophone – has started up to produce these compact models, and the larger established firms have also been introducing hand-portable models.

The total world market for cellular telephones is currently around 2.5 million units installed, with annual growth rates around 40 per cent. The US market alone is estimated to be worth between \$4 and \$5 bn by 1990.

Other forms of terminal equipment associated with the growth of new networks include pagers and videotex equipment for interactive cable. The former is already commonplace but is still undergoing rapid growth. The latter is quite restricted, is still subject to considerable uncertainty, and as yet remains more within the specialised consumer audio industry.

Paging equipment has traditionally been seen as peripheral to telecommunications partly due to its radio one-way operation, and also because it has until recently involved no information exchange save for an alerting signal. Three elements of change are affecting this perception. Firstly, increased technical sophistication within the paging network allows a greater information content to be transmitted. The advent of cellular technology has had a knock-on effect for paging in that national and even international networks can be utilised more effectively using this technology, with short messages being transmitted rather than a single signal. Secondly, sophistication within the pager allows several different means of receiving information. Thus small displays are already available, messages can be stored and recalled, and one-way or even two-way voice systems will become available in the future.

A third important issue is that, with digital operation, local paging systems can be directly interfaced with the PABX giving direct access for other subscribers to call up pager numbers without operator intervention. Pagers may therefore also be linked direct to alarm and control systems, telephone answering machines or voice message systems.

In addition to terminals for new networks, there have been a number of innovations in the terminals attached to the existing network. Many are more sophisticated adaptations of existing products, such as complex telephones

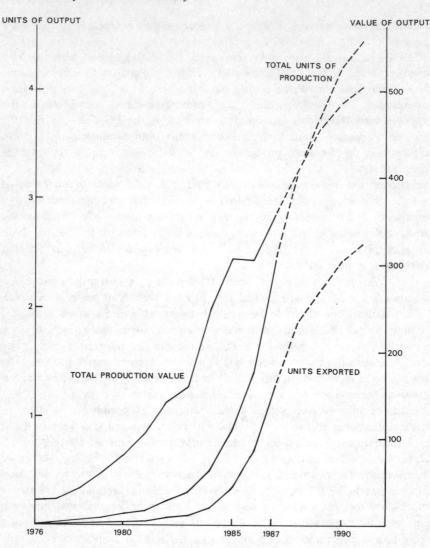

Figure 3.3 Japanese production of facsimile machines

and personal-computer-based terminals. The most significant new product is, however, a completely new concept in the office environment, although in an earlier form it had been in specialist use for many years: the facsimile machine.

Particularly high growth has been seen in the market for facsimile machines (fax) especially in the last three years as a critical mass has been reached. This growth can be illustrated by Figure 3.3, showing unit output of fax within Japan, which makes up a majority of world production.

The origins of fax lie in the transmission of newspaper articles and photographs. The technology initially came from a British firm, Muirhead, in 1947. Throughout the period to 1980 Muirhead concentrated on that one sophisticated market, supplying machines to transmit whole pages to dispersed printing centres and holding a 90 per cent world market share for most of the period (*Guardian* 21.6.84).

The development of the market for facsimile machines illustrates two major principles in new communications product introduction: standardisation and critical mass. The utility of telecommunications products depends upon their market penetration. One terminal is useless; two allow communication; many allow multiple communications.

Prior to the rapid uptake of fax by Japanese producers in the late 1970s a number of US manufacturers produced for a niche market of fax networks – primarily in the news media and intra-corporate organisations. Many differing standards existed, with manufacturers often changing protocols over time, between models. Communication between machines of different origins and models was impossible. A buyer would install a complete network, then update on a total-replacement rather than evolutionary basis.

In contrast, Japanese producers were driven by the need for interfirm communication, partly because of the problems of transmitting text containing Kanji symbols by other means. The CCITT standards set in the late 1970s were therefore adopted by the Japanese giving the downwardly compatible groups I, II, III and IV standards. Thus all group III machines (the most common available) can communicate, regardless of model or make; and they can all communicate with group II machines at a slower transmission rate. Thus with this standardisation the fax became a commodity product enabling rapid sales growth.

As sales grew, the wide distribution of machines stimulated further usage and adoption. As a firm's customers and suppliers bought and utilised fax for transaction documents, pressure was exerted on non-adopters also to make use of fax. This was particularly reinforced by the economic benefits that could be realised, and by the potential competitive disadvantages of non-adoption. Where formerly documents might require an expensive overnight courier service, fax can replace this service with cheaper delivery in minutes. In telex also, Western Union of the USA report that fax has led to a reduction of US telex traffic from 397 million minutes per annum in 1984 to 200 million minutes per annum in 1987. NTT estimates that half of all telephone traffic between the USA and Japan is fax (*Business Week*, 1988).

In response to the domination of the world fax market by the Japanese (with over 90 per cent share) most European and North American firms have resorted to OEM deals. One ambitious attempt to break this trend came from Federal Express, the US courier firm, who were losing business to fax. Their Zap Mail system employed a network of group IV machines, sourced from NEC, linked by satellite. Federal Express would rent the machines to customers gaining revenues from rental and from utilisation of the dedicated network. Three problems emerged. Firstly, the high quality Zap mailer was considerably more expensive than group III fax and few firms felt that the quality justified the cost difference. Secondly, the lack of compatibility with group III machines connected to the public telephone network restricted usage. Thirdly, those firms that really needed fax already had group III machines and saw no need to switch to a new arbitrary network standard. Zap mail was abandoned after two years in which it lost $300 million. (*Business*, 1987).

The TSE industry

The TSE industry is generally dominated by large integrated telecommunications manufacturers, although with some encroachment from new entrants from two sources: the data processing/office automation industry and the consumer-electronics industry. A small number of firms are also integrated manufacturers and service providers. This includes the world's largest telecommunications firm AT & T. In other service providers the manufacturing arm is relatively small scale, as in British Telecom and Televerket (in Sweden). Another US service provider (GTE) recently sold off its TSE division to Fujitsu, one of the four largest telecommunications firms in Japan.

Few TSE firms are organised on a genuinely international level with the exception of Alcatel and IBM, although others may export a considerable share of their output. This is largely a legacy of the past regulatory framework and is now being overcome as a number of firms make overseas investments or acquisitions in order to compete in the new environment.

Three tiers of firms were identified within the TSE industry. The global players in TSE are essentially the telecommunication giants: AT & T, Alcatel, Siemens, Northern Telecom, Ericsson, NEC and potentially IBM. Other Japanese firms may graduate to this grouping in future, although, with the exception of facsimile, their overseas presence has been limited as yet.

Below this upper tier lie a number of firms that are significant in the home markets with some international sales or else have been successful in niche markets. This grouping takes in the other large Japanese firms, Fujitsu, Oki, Hitachi, Toshiba; European firms such as GPT, STC, Italtel, Telenorma, Matra, Nixdorf, Philips; and North American firms including Harris and Mitel.

Finally, the small domestic or niche producers would typically include Nitsuko, Iwatsu, Teli, Ferranti, Technophone, Orbitel, Krone, De Te We.

Within the UK the three major domestic telecommunications producers have been GEC, Plessey and STC. In 1988 the telecommunication activities of GEC and Plessey were merged into a joint venture (GPT). STC has had a more convoluted history in recent years. It began as a subsidiary of ITT, gaining relative independence through flotation, bought ICL (the only UK mainframe computer manufacturer), then had ITT's holding of 25 per cent transferred to Northern Telecom. Other UK-owned producers include relatively new entrants such as Ferranti, Racal and Technophone. Additionally, the UK has seen inward investment both historically, from Philips (in TMC) and more recently by Motorola, NEC and Ericsson.

The German telecommunications industry is dominated by Siemens, a global player, but there are also a number of smaller firms. Alcatel is represented through Standard Electric Lorenz. Other large German electronics firms with telecoms divisions include AEG, Robert Bosch (with Telenorma) and Nixdorf. Philips also has a subsidiary, Te Ka De. The Bundespost and the larger firms also support a number of small firms and subcontractors, including Krone and De Te We.

France contrasts with Germany in that the industry has already undergone dramatic restructuring and hence within the indigenous sector industrial concentration is high. The major event was the merging of the telecommunications activities of OGE and Thomson within CGE Alcatel. The later merging of the ITT businesses into this group had little effect in France as the French ITT subsidiary had been nationalised previously. This firm, CGCT, was later sold off in a fiercely competed contest, the winner of which was a consortium of Matra and Ericsson. Matra is currently the second largest French-owned producer and has been particularly strong in cellular technology. Finally, there are a number of foreign-owned firms including the Jeumont Schneider group now owned by Bosch.

In Scandanavia the dominant force is Ericsson, and other firms tend to operate in partnership with them. Thus in Sweden, Teli, the subsidiary of Televerket, undertakes joint development of switching products and in Norway, Elektrisk Bureau (formerly an affiliate of Ericsson) manufactures Ericsson exchanges under licence. Nokia of Finland is also emerging as a strong participant in certain sectors, notably in cellular communications.

In North America the main protaganists are AT & T with its Western Electric subsidiary (now part of AT & T Technologies) and Northern Telecom in Canada. Other leading firms have been acquired or have sold off their TSE interests. However a number of smaller independents such as Harris and Comdial remain including ITT, GTE and Mitel with domestic interests mainly. PABX and data products are also produced by computer firms of which there are a large number, including some specialist new firms.

IBM appears determined to be a major force in the TSE industry, adding the PABX manufacturer Rolm to its own communications activities in 1984. The strength of IBM lies in its dominant world position in the computer industry which gives it a network of manufacturing plants, marketing and sales forces and an existing relationship through installed equipment with many firms. IBM has the capacity to manufacture and market any new product at a global scale, with potential economies of scale and scope. With its considerable installed base of computer equipment IBM is also in an inside position when competing for communications orders – especially when data communications are significant. Despite this, IBM has still found difficulty in marketing telecommunications products and its presence in most markets is still small compared with other global firms and large domestic firms. One should not, however, underestimate a firm which has penetrated most key markets as IBM has done, even if its share in these markets is relatively small.

The Japanese TSE industry has traditionally been dominated by the four NTT family companies: NEC, Hitachi, Fujitsu and Oki. All four are diversified companies, although Oki is somewhat smaller than the other three. NEC, Hitachi and Fujitsu are global competitors in a wide range of products including all aspects of communications, computers and components. (Hitachi's products, for example range from integrated circuits to large-scale excavation equipment to nuclear power stations.) Nevertheless all four firms regard telecommunications as a key market sector in conjunction with computer technology. Aside from these firms there are a number of smaller telecommunications specialists such as Iwatsu, Nitsuko and Tamura who may have operated as subcontractors in the past, but now increasingly supply NTT directly. Also now a number of larger firms from the consumer electronics sector are moving into telecommunications, particularly the TSE sectors (for example Sony, Matsushita, Canon, Toshiba, Sharp and Ricoh).

Global alliances

Despite the large size of the major firms in the telecommunications industry, there has been a marked growth in collaborations, joint ventures and other non-competitive arrangements. Some of these collaborations are supported by public policy, either directly – as in the case of European R & D programmes ESPRIT, RACE and so on – or indirectly, as in the relaxation of anti-trust regulation in the USA. Many agreements are purely commercial relationships orientated towards market penetration while others aim at the fullest exploitation of a technology or production base, or the synergetic harnessing of comparative strengths between the partners.

One of the incentives for such ventures comes from the difficulty of market penetration due to regulatory barriers. Thus a firm may seek a relatively weak local partner to act as an indigenous supplier of equipment based upon the technology and knowhow of the former. However, there are a number of examples where this is obviously not the case and the external and internal forces and benefits are more complex. These will be developed in the following chapters, but at this stage it is useful to categorise alliances and indicate the level of activity and apparent trends.

Intercompany collaboration can be categorised in several ways. One can describe them in terms of linkages (horizontal, vertical), type of activity (basic research, development, production) or institutional basis (long term, short term, equity holdings, agreements, licences etc). In addition, public sector partners may also be involved, such as universities, PTTs, government industrial-research facilities or a government department sponsoring industry or research.

Hakansson (1987) uses a threefold classification to describe linkage/competitive relationships between industrial collaborators:

- Vertical cooperation involving seller–buyer relationships.
- Horizontal competitive cooperation involving firms that normally compete directly, collaborating either on a specific project for which they recognise the need for greater resources or a structured market, or in basic research at a pre-competitive stage.
- Horizontal complementary cooperation involving firms that may supply different but complementary products within a broadly defined market where the advantage lies in the scope of marketing effort or the application of technology across a broader product range.

In each of these areas there are clear examples of collaboration in TSE. Seller–buyer cooperation focuses primarily on the supply of semiconductor components and there are a number of working relationships particularly with the custom IC manufacturers. In addition, more diverse relationships exist between groups of telecommunication firms and their internal semiconductor divisions as well as with third-party suppliers. New VLSI chips for ISDN for example are being designed and specified within such vertical–horizontal groupings.

Horizontal competitive cooperation has developed between a number of firms who have been seeking to reduce the costs of developing expensive new technology and in some cases basic systems. The most typical case would be the licensing of a product, but often the competitive element may be suppressed by deals over markets. It is rare that one finds two firms selling identical, jointly developed products in competition with each other. This has happened in recent years in the UK, due mainly to British Telecom's distortion in the market by jointly designing products with two or more manufacturers in order to introduce competition and second sources for a standard product. However, with the merger of GEC's and Plessey's telecommunication businesses and the withdrawal of BT from this type of joint development programme such arrangements are likely to become less frequent.

Complementary cooperation is probably the most common type of alliance, encompassing as it does OEM deals, computer-telecommunications link-ups and many of the collaborations between smaller manufacturers or between mainstream TSE-product firms and niche firms. In many cases, a long-term collaboration between horizontal competitive firms will develop into this complementary model as market agreements are made and specialisation within each firm occurs to maximise benefits of the coupling. The Northern Telecom–STC link up or the ATT–Olivetti collaboration are two typical cases where the product ranges are distinct and, due to equity holdings, the relationships will be long term with complementarity expected to increase over time.

In addition to describing collaboration in terms of linkage or competitive relations between the firms, the collaboration can also be classified according to the nature of the specific project or relationship (Sharp and Shearman, 1987). Thus collaboration between competitive firms on a horizontal basis could be a pre-competitive sharing of basic research, a product development project or an OEM or licensing deal. A second classification on this basis is presented below as a complement to the first. The two classifications may be viewed as a two-dimensional matrix with each collaboration being defined by the relationship between the firms and the nature or objective of the collaboration project.

- Pre-competitive R & D cooperation:
  - co-funded research centres, for example Bellcore;
  - university-based industry-funded R & D;
  - government–industry collaborative projects, for example RACE;
  - venture capital provided by two or more corporations for component supplies eg, ES^2; and
  - cooperation on standards, for example for ISDN through CCITT.
- Product development cooperation:
  - non-equity project-specific agreements;
  - joint ventures for specific product areas eg. Orbitel; and
  - PTT-manufacturer(s) procurement-related projects, for example System X.
- Manufacturing/marketing cooperation:
  - OEM agreements – numerous examples;
  - cross-equity linkages, for example Northern Telecom–STC;
  - full-range joint ventures, for example Thorn-Ericsson; and
  - licensing of existing products – numerous examples.

Collaboration also varies according to the product or component concerned. Thus for a TSE manufacturer the range of technologies with which they need to be familiar is extremely broad at the component or system-component level (see Figure 3.4). Contrastingly, the putting-together of a full PABX system from assorted devices is essentially a software problem. Thus at a technical level collaboration is required to enable firms to cope with the lack of scale and scope in component technologies. Internalisation is often undesirable due to the low level of value added in this area compared with applications. However, despite the obvious desire to capture the full benefits of value added at the application end of production, market-penetration problems may require collaboration here also.

Within Europe, Ericsson has been particularly active in alliance formation

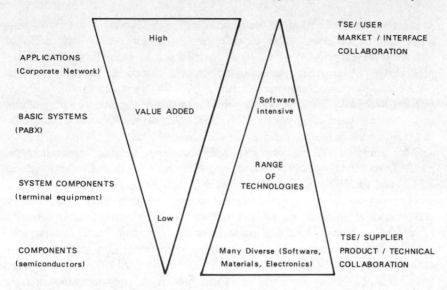

Figure 3.4 Relationship between technology and value added in TSE

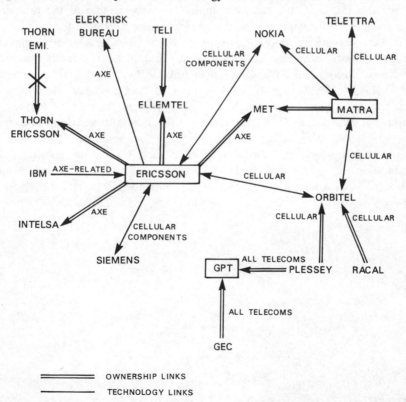

Figure 3.5 Network of relationships between Ericsson, Matra and GPT

as a prelude to the creation of the Single European Market, despite the firm's home country, Sweden, lying outside the Community. Two main areas of technological expertise have emerged at the core of these links (see Figure 3.5). Firstly, the AXE public exchange, developed in conjunction with Televerket, is now being manufactured by joint ventures in the UK and France. Secondly, Ericsson has acquired substantial expertise in the cellular telecommunications field which forms the basis of a consortium to develop the pan-European digital cellular network into the 1990s.

Other European firms have also been active in forming such alliances, partly encouraged by the actions of the European Commission, through its RACE and ESPRIT collaborative research programmes. The continued movement towards a European-scale internal market has also led to collaboration and merger at an international and national level. Member states, formerly concerned with high levels of ownership concentration, have relaxed anti-trust legislation in recognition of greater international competition and the scale requirements of telecommunications productions. In some cases mergers have been actively encouraged, as in the French industry reorganisation. In the UK the GEC–Plessey telecommunications joint venture was encouraged by government, despite a ban on complete merger because of the prospects of a reduction of competitive tendering for defence equipment.

At an international level there have been considerable developments between North American and European firms, most recently between Northern Telecom and STC. Other such links include British Telecom/Mitel and CGE/ITT. However, TSE is less affected than associated technologies such as main switching products (ATT/Philips) and computers (numerous examples). Within the USA and Japan, collaboration seems less developed than in Europe. With regard for standards the Japanese have a much more coordinated approach, as can be seen from their successful capture of the facsimile market partly through standardisation. Failure to collaborate in this way has led American fax manufacturers to turn to OEM deals for survival.

4 Economies of Scale in TSE Production

Firms' scale of operation

The existence of some benefits from scale of operation or size of firm in the telecommunications industry may appear self-evident: there are high levels of concentration, firms are of large absolute size and there is a continuing tendency for merger and collaboration between firms. However, in view of the practical problems of measuring the benefits of 'pure' economies of scale, the issue must be approached from a wider perspective than has been adopted in other economic studies. The present study sought to determine:

- The current scale of production of the firms for specific TSE products.
- The necessary or desirable scale of production as perceived by the firms.
- The specific forces and elements determining these production levels.
- The means of realising potential benefits and of overcoming problems that might occur as a consequence of lack of sufficient size.

The absence of open homogenous markets for telecommunications products introduces considerable national differentials into firms' cost and price structures, and this is compounded currently by the coexistence of several different product and process technologies. Generally, the newer product and component technologies provide a more favourable cost:performance ratio. Yet older technologies persist, due to inertia in the provision of infrastructure, or in the delayed writing-off and replacement of existing private-network equipment. These market distortions can considerably affect the potential for scale economies. Nevertheless, most firms were very aware of scale requirements, and more specifically could explore the nature of their cost structures and the effect of scale in specific elements of their operations.

In determining the scale of production of manufactured items, there are two options open to the researcher. Firstly, the value of output can be measured in monetary terms. This can be influenced by the variation in the product but is particularly useful for comparisons of fixed costs. For example, if there were minimum costs of capital investment, development and setting up a distribution network, their cost in relation to total turnover would indicate particular constraints. Secondly, the absolute number of units of output could be compared. This might relate to the minimum economic purchasing volume of components, the throughput of specific machines or the volume of output demanded by monopsonistic customers.

The relationship between these two measures is of course not constant over time, or between firms. Higher volumes lead to lower unit costs, but unit costs are falling in real terms over time for other reasons also, and product segmentation and differentiation is high. However, despite these problems a number of general observations can be made which cast light on the potential benefits of large-scale production within the industry. In general, data on volume of production (in units) was most readily available and is the primary measure used, although the difference between assessing volume of discrete terminals and of complete PABX systems will become clear.

Telephone production

Telephone production is typically a large-scale assembly process. PTT orders are generally in terms of hundreds of thousands and in some cases long-term orders may run to over a million units. Unit costs have been driven down very keenly as a consequence of competitive bidding and liberalisation. The reduction in number of components and assembly time has become very marked in recent years and, despite the embodying of advanced component technology in the telephone, it has become a mature electronic consumer product.

Almost all manufacturers producing basic handsets for standard PTT domestic/office use are currently looking for minimum volumes in excess of a million units per annum. In Europe, production volumes in the range of 1 to 1.5 million sets were standard for firms which otherwise varied in size. Smaller producers with a limited range of products were therefore needing to gear up to this level of volume to maintain competitiveness. Three European firms were found to be producing over this level, one of which, Alcatel, is the world's largest telephone producer and produced several times more than the next largest European, although with production distributed between several national subsidiaries.

The major US manufacturers were also producing over the 'minimum level' with predictably high volumes from industry leaders such as AT & T. The leading Japanese firms were producing at levels similar to those of the medium-sized European firms. However, given the Communication Industry Association of Japan's estimate of around 10 million sets of annual production in Japan, the second tier firms must be producing at much smaller levels.

The level of production achieved by the leading NIC producers also conforms to this pattern. The major Taiwanese firms appear to be achieving production levels of the order of several millions per annum headed by one firm with an estimated 5 million sets. The vast majority of the 20 million plus telephones produced in Taiwan are exported, principally to the US and to the liberalised EC markets.

Exceptions to this general industry level of one million sets fall into two groups of firms. Firstly there are the small niche or subcontract producers who can operate in the margins left by the major manufacturers. Some are making specialised sets to be sold at a premium, based upon styling or function, for which there is a small but inelastic market. Others are involved in general subcontract work using designs and components specified elsewhere.

The second group includes firms whose primary TSE business is PABX but who also produce specialised telephone terminals to be sold as part of turnkey systems. The economics of manufacturing and selling PABX terminals are sufficiently different from those of telephones to allow for smaller levels of production, although this opportunity may disappear as turnkey PABX system prices in all countries fall to the price levels of the most liberalised markets.

The crucial elements determining minimum scale of telephone production appear to be components and, to a lesser extent, the sharing of overheads such as design and marketing.

PABX production

In considering minimum scale in PABX assembly, a short description of the nature of the difference in product compared with telephones – and its effect on scale – is useful.

Production volumes of PABX can be measured in terms of numbers of lines, that is the number of internal line circuits provided within a given number of systems manufactured. (Thus if a firm makes a PABX with provision for 50 outside lines and 1000 internal extensions this is counted as 1000 lines towards total production.) Historically, this measure emerged because each line was a distinct circuit wired separately into the frame of the exchange. Current-generation digital PABX will have several line circuits on each printed circuit board. Each is still a recognisable entity and, as the basis of the system, is the mass replicated element. Thus a system may be of 300 or 3000 lines, but to achieve this it will require first and foremost a multitude of the line-circuit units.

Firms in the sample were asked to give an indication of production levels both in terms of numbers of lines and in total output. This does not, however, take into account the number of models and size ranges of exchanges. If each exchange requires a minimum volume of production, then a firm supplying six different models will not be comparable in total output terms with one supplying just one model. Accepting this caveat, the production volumes of the firms sampled ranged from around 150,000 lines pa to 2 million lines pa.

Three tiers of firm could be identified. Firstly, there were a number of small-scale manufacturers with volumes of around 200,000 lines pa. These could be found in virtually all countries and were usually supplying limited ranges, often of small exchanges and key phones. They tended to be primarily aimed at domestic markets only and often licensed their products from large overseas suppliers. Secondly, a middle tier of firms could be described as 'national champions', with a production level of around 500,000 lines, a more comprehensive range of products and in some cases extensive exports. These firms were capable of designing their own systems but were still involved in some collaborative arrangements. Thirdly, the very largest firms in the range of around 1 million lines pa, or greater, were able to manufacture at an international level and compete in every segment of the market.

The study sample necessarily focused on the larger firms, which make up a large proportion of total industry output, but a number of quite small suppliers exist on the margin supplying essentially niche markets. This is indicative of the nature of the scale requirements within the PABX market. The critical issue for most firms was not the manufacturing or component issues so much as overheads in the form of R & D, marketing and sales. Thus to be able to compete in all market segments, with a wide range of PABXs, with all new interfaces and facilities, requires very high R & D costs and a large marketing and sales effort. Nevertheless, it is possible for smaller firms to coexist in the short term by concentrating on small, less complex systems, licensing in PABXs or system components and using independent sales organisations for distribution. This is feasible particularly if sales can be supported by or channelled through PTTs (especially in non-liberalised markets) or through large national distributors of telecommunication products which are independent of other manufacturers. However, such strategies may not be adequate in the long term, without a close alliance with one of the larger firms or groupings.

Cost reductions in manufacturing are not totally accounted for by scale economies however. Three elements to cost reductions may be identified which may be simultaneously or independently effective.

- Straightforward economies of scale may be obtained by an increased level of production, yielding more efficient use of capital, higher discounts on components and a greater spreading of fixed costs, among other factors.
- Learning benefits may be achieved in the short term by minor alterations to products or processes to increase the efficiency of the manufacturing process, eliminating bottlenecks, designing out recurrent flaws and so on. On a longer time-scale this continual evolutionary change may include the replacement of components with cheaper or fewer alternatives which can lead to quite dramatic cost reductions but also considerable changes in the product.
- Economies of scale within the component supplier's industry and competitive price cutting may lead to falling component costs independent of volume of purchase or substitution (or learning). These cost reductions may be absorbed by profits or passed directly on to customers, without changes to manufacturing. Rapidly falling component costs may in some cases lead to delays in other forms

of saving, by increased volume or technological change, unless competitors engage in keen price cutting or product-differentiation strategies.

The manufacturing dimension

The neoclassical concept of scale economies is based on the realisation of cost savings by the scaling up of manufacturing operations and hence the use of more efficient machines and processes. However, for any manufacturing technology there will effectively be an engineering optimum or maximum capacity for a particular machine. Thus on a pure engineering basis, scale economies will only apply over a size range up to this maximum scale. Above this, capital indivisibility problems set in, but the problem becomes a management rather than an engineering problem. For example, if a machine for producing a million units is more efficient than smaller versions, then production levels of less than a million will be subject to higher costs. Similarly, above a million units engineering diseconomies will occur until 2 million units are achieved, allowing the use of two machines at their optimally efficient rate.

This rather simple engineering notion, however, has little resemblance to reality. A particular engineering function, such as component insertion, will in reality be performed by a number of machines with differing capacities and cost:performance ratios. The firm will aim to select an economic machine, but will probably be aware that it will not be utilised to its full – unless the capital cost of the machine was a very large proportion of total costs.

The realisation of economies of scale in manufacturing operations depends on the extent to which capacity is utilised. If one were to estimate that the optimum scale of manufacturing telephones was 2 million pa, and that this required a dedicated plant, then 50 per cent utilisation would clearly present problems. In reality, in the telecommunications industry, capacity of plant is rarely fixed; a certain level of capital may be installed, but its utilisation may be variable over time depending upon labour usage. In most cases, the existing plant is not being run on a 24-hour basis, so allowing for some slack, and forming the basis for some upward flexibility in output. If growth in output is required on a long-term basis, then selective capital investment may also be made to eliminate bottlenecks allowing volume to creep up. In some cases large step-function increases may be required, but this is rarer than incremental change. It was suggested by several major firms in the USA and Europe that dedicated automated plants inhibited volume flexibility, so that the likelihood of diseconomies in times of under or over utilisation might outweigh the economies of scale whilst operating at the optimal level. If the potential savings from dedicated plants are very small with respect to total costs then there is little incentive to risk diseconomies from under utilisation.

This trade-off between optimal utilisation in the engineering sense and volume flexibility was perceived by most firms. Generally, at least 10 per cent of capacity was reserved for sudden demand surges. One exception to this pattern was a European firm which relied on subcontractors to cope with peaks in demand, but this partly reflected their history of employment growth in telecommunications after a relatively recent entry to the sector. This firm had never experienced overmanning due to demand falls or technical change, and had not been in a position to establish a normal output and employment level at less than previous maxima. By contrast, in most other firms some labour reductions had occurred, offering a source of temporary labour to cope with short-term production increases.

Most of the firms in Europe and the USA viewed the manufacturing function as a fixed overhead with regard to capital and permanent labour (although with some flexibility in the latter). This cost therefore needed to be covered by revenue from production throughput, and it was dependent upon the marketing and sales departments to maximise sales and so spread these costs most widely. The efficiency gains were, however, judged by some firms to be less significant than savings in component costs through bulk purchasing and, related to this, savings in inventory costs by reducing work in progress and stockpiled goods. In PABX, in particular, the low priority given to simple engineering economies of scale was well illustrated by the number of firms operating small overseas assembly plants, with the scale-sensitive R & D and component-sourcing functions being centralised within the parent establishment.

The supply of components

The cost of components is the major element in the manufacturing costs of subscriber equipment with around 60 to 70 per cent of factory-gate costs being attributable to components and materials. Clearly therefore, cost savings in this area are most significant for total savings and hence for competitive pricing. There are several elements to these potential savings, and a number of different strategies by which they may be achieved. The most significant elements are electronic components, specifically integrated circuits. There are also a number of electrical or physical components: handset capsules, power supplies, casings and so on which are of lower importance, but which cannot be neglected.

All firms reported a reduction in component costs with increased volumes, but most felt that in their particular case the issue was not significant at a marginal level. With levels of telephone production of over a million pa it was presumed by most firms that to achieve significant marginal savings would require massive increases in capacity of an unrealistic nature. For standard electronic components it appears that discount level prices can be achieved with the typical levels of output of most firms in the survey.

Some firms were able to estimate the rates of discount available at lower volume levels of purchasing. One European firm, for example, claimed that a doubling of size of order gave a 20 per cent discount, although this discount was only applied at very small volumes. A UK firm suggested that 4.5 per cent discount was the usual reduction for a doubling of order size. If these savings were significant, it therefore implied that the firm was too small to be competitive. The only time when changes in discount on prices mattered was during the start-up phase of production. For high-volume manufacturers, with perhaps 30–40 per cent national market share, a doubling of output to gain a 2 per cent overall cost saving was not a practical suggestion.

Volume discounts for standard components, whether used in a wide number of industries or widely used within telecommunications, may be somewhat misleading in any case, due to the low cost and rapid non-volume discounting that has occurred (UNCTC, 1986). Year-on-year falls in the price of semiconductors are likely to be much more significant to the firm than small marginal changes in price due to volume.

There was a feeling among a small group of firms that European firms would always be disadvantaged with regard to component prices compared with the firms in South East Asia. However other European firms felt that they were able to buy on an equal basis, and one UK firm reported that they were buying semiconductor components at a lower price than some Asian competitors.

The price of application-specific integrated circuits (ASICs) was more sensitive to size of order as these might be limited in availability to one or a small grouping of firms. The demand for use of ASICs comes from two pressures. On the one hand it was reported that there is a technical need in interfacing between analogue and digital signals, for example when interfacing old analogue telephone lines with digital or ISDN switches. The second demand arises out of the need for further degrees of integration in order to reduce costs by the elimination of components and reduction of assembly time. Several IC and discrete components may be replaced by a more complex IC which is specifically designed for the product or product range. In most cases the ASIC will be more expensive than other individual components, but the price is usually less than that of the several components it replaces, providing the volume required is large enough. Thus four standard ICs at £1 each may be effectively replaced by an ASIC at £2.50.

Because ASICs are produced at relatively low volume, unit costs will be higher, although the technological advances in chip design allow for a semi-custom approach, where only the later design stages are customised, and the chip is built from a standard format or gate array. Nevertheless there are considerable costs for the design of the device which must be spread across a smaller total output than that of 'merchant' chips. These design costs are, however, much smaller than the design costs for a totally custom-built device. The cost of designing and implementing a semi-custom device was estimated to be of the order of £200,000.

The decision to use ASICs, however, is not dependent solely on cost considerations. There may be strategic benefits to be gained from particular functions incorporated into the device. The firm therefore has a number of trade-offs to make in deciding on an ASIC alternative, not all of which are totally related to procurement cost savings. For example, particular functions which are a source of competitive advantage in product differentiation may only be elegantly achieved by using custom devices. Also, niche markets may exist for small products, where integration is essential for space saving, and where prices and hence costs would not necessarily have to be as low as for standard products. However, once a decision is made to choose a particular type of component attempts to reduce costs may be sought.

Several different options are available to the firm in seeking a reduction in the cost of ASICs, or indeed of standard components, all of which involve a sharing out of fixed costs or a pooling of purchasing power.

Four strategies were used by TSE firms to secure reductions in the cost of components.

Interfirm consortia

There were many cases of firms which grouped together their purchasing power by setting up joint procurement offices or by jointly specifying custom devices. Two procurement consortia were identified in Europe, each bringing together firms from more than one country. A Swedish manager explained that the purchasing power of such a consortium was the only means of obtaining the reduced costs on standard components that would otherwise be achieved by the doubling or quadrupling of purchasing, through corresponding increases of output. Competitiveness requires savings on component costs, which are a large proportion of total costs, but with significant marginal savings requiring enormous changes in output these were not available without collaboration.

For the reduction of costs of ASICs, procurement was less significant than joint specification. The savings were due to the higher scale of production of what would be customer-specified devices. So the user firms would gain from production economies of scale in the component supplier, and TSE firms savings from the pooling of design resources and costs. Such ASIC consortia are becoming commonplace, emerging from collaborative IT programmes in Europe, Japan and the USA.

Joint specification

A less formal arrangement, joint specification of components may be undertaken – sometimes surreptitiously without the knowledge of all purchasers. For instance, a small firm may place an order with a component supplier for a device that is being sourced by a larger firm without the large firm knowing of the order. One UK firm had chosen to use a device which was being sourced from an independent supplier by another European firm. This IC was for a specific application, but was proprietary to the supplier rather than the users. A particular benefit expected by the UK firm was the continuity of supply due to the buying power of the European firm. However, it transpired that the European firm switched its sourcing arrangements without the knowledge of the UK firm, so increasing the risk to the UK firm which was then the only user of that device. This illustrates the potential dangers of such informal arrangements.

User–supplier collaboration

Collaboration also occurs between users and suppliers. One European firm had established a close working relationship with an ASIC manufacturer and arranged for joint funding of development costs. In return for its investment in a particular device, the ASIC supplier could market the product to third parties. The interests of the user however were protected by a six-to-nine-months exclusive right to purchase all output. Thus the TSE manufacturer could gain some competitive advantage from the use of a custom designed IC, but without the full costs of development, and without sharing access to the design with competitors during the crucial early stages of use.

Intra-firm procurement coordination

A fourth means of achieving scale economies in purchasing is through joint procurement with other divisions of the firm. One German firm used components from computer systems within telecommunications products, and the majority of firms in the study had established interdivisional purchasing groups or committees. This mode of operation, however, falls within the economies of scope in the use of shareable inputs and is a good illustration of the convergence of the scale and scope benefits.

Component sourcing is one example of the close interrelations between economies of scale and scope. Many of the larger, vertically integrated firms gain advantages from in-house component supply (see Chapter 5). However if the TSE division is perceived to be a key market for a new component, the feasibility of the new investment may depend upon the scale of TSE use. So, for example, it may be advantageous for a firm to source 1 megabit memory devices internally in order to internalise technical benefits and gain entry to that component market. In order to justify the high level of investment and continuous volume production required for IC manufacture, this may imply that a certain level of demand is needed from internal customers such as the TSE division. Inadequate scale of demand in the end-user division may therefore jeopardise the component-production investment by undermining its viability and hence the ability of the firm to realise scope benefits in both cost and technical terms.

Another scale-related issue links components with national standards. Each of the major developed markets has slightly different requirements for the external interfaces for PABX. Thus a family of custom ICs may be needed in order to be able to supply global markets. One solution is to design a basic custom IC which can be reconfigured for each national standard at the final stage of manufacture. For example, one German firm suggested that it would begin with the German version, then develop devices compatible, say, with the UK and US standards in order to sell into those markets. The fourth version of the IC would then probably be the world-market version (CCITT standard) which is adopted by most small European markets (for example, Portugal, Turkey) and by Third-World markets. Current liberalisation policies are aimed at minimising these market barriers, but for the immediate future there are still likely to be costs associated with national standards that require large size of firm to enable entry. One UK firm estimated it could cost £5 million to customise a PABX for another market.

All the larger firms had recognised the importance of economies of scale in component purchasing, particularly for telephone and terminal production. Most were purchasing at levels which gave considerable discounts, and therefore smaller competitors were severely disadvantaged. Further scale increases for the larger firms might yield marginal savings, but such increases were not generally available because of the current industrial structure. However, firms also stressed other factors in the use of components, manufacturing technology and product design which interlinked with purchasing economies. Thus the exhaustion of potential economies of scale was seen to be a necessary but not sufficient condition for long-term survival in the mainstream TSE industry.

Marketing and sales

Telecommunications-equipment marketing is a relatively new concept in many countries, where, until recently, regulation and state monopoly have determined the distribution of TSE. With the general move to more open markets for many TSE products, firms have needed to establish sales and service networks, and to devote more resources to marketing. The implications of this are considerable. Many firms had been used to receiving development and production contracts direct from the PTT, which had been responsible for demand forecasting, some R & D and design, distribution and after-sales service. In their new role as competitor and supplier to the PTT, manufacturers had to acquire the capability of undertaking all these additional roles and functions formerly undertaken by the PTT, often within the difficult environment of falling domestic market share and price cutting.

Two questions with respect to scale are therefore important to consider. Firstly, in such a turbulent period, were larger scale firms, as a consequence of their financial resources, more able to weather these pressures and quickly commit resources to develop marketing and sales functions? Secondly, to what extent do marketing and sales act as fixed costs to be amortised over expanding scale of total sales, and are there economies of scale internal to these functions? Precise data on these issues are difficult to obtain, but evidence can be presented to demonstrate the importance of firm size on these aspects of the firms' operations.

It is important to recognise that in some cases the functions of sales and marketing were already partly developed as a consequence of firms' international operations. So even though domestic markets may have been regulated and controlled, overseas markets – particularly in the Third World and smaller countries – were more open due to the absence of indigenous suppliers. Several firms have a long-established presence in such markets and have global networks of production, marketing and sales. For example, ITT, Siemens and Ericsson had already adopted a market-led approach in the more open markets, in advance of liberalisation in the larger core markets. This global presence brought both scale and a more adaptable corporate organisation although it is clear that a market-led structure was not a consequence of scale but was a factor in its achievement.

Firms having to move into a more market-led mode of operations than previously have met several constraints. Firstly, market trends have been difficult to predict on the basis of previous information, due to the discontinuities in industry structure, and rapid growth induced either by pre-liberalisation actions on the part of PTTs (for example, BT's PABX sales influx) or post-liberalisation growth. Secondly, the dominant role of the PTT in supplying equipment may persist, especially in domestic TSE supply as opposed to business systems. The firm in this case would be torn between attempting to maintain good relations with the PTT to maximise its share of that distribution network, and setting up a competing distribution network or supplying another competitor to the PTT. As the share of the market held by the PTT must decline to some extent with liberalisation – due to the entry of new competition – relying purely on the PTT as a distributor is likely to reduce the possibility for sales growth in that market.

With regard to the ownership and organisation of a sales network, there are a number of options which may be pursued. Firstly the firm may create a large integrated sales force within the TSE production division. Secondly it may set up a separately accountable sales division with an integrated structure. Thirdly it may decentralise its sales division into spatially defined profit centres, and fourthly it may handle all sales activities through one or more third parties.

At an international level, more than one structure may be adopted within an individual firm, although it is less desirable to have such co-existence within national markets, and most firms have avoided dual structures where possible.

Another dimension of this issue is the extent to which the sales network is dedicated to the TSE products of one company. Some sales organisations of TSE firms sell products from other firms to complement the internally supplied range, whereas in the case of third-party sales organisations they may additionally wish to offer alternatives to customers. Another means of increasing the number of products sold by an existing sales network is to broaden its remit to include, for example, networking equipment or office equipment – again a link between scale and scope benefits.

Scale and R & D

A major issue particularly relevant to public policy, competition and firm strategies is the recognition of the existence of minimum feasible R & D levels or thresholds, and the change in such thresholds over time. At an absolute minimum a TSE firm would need to be able to design a simple terminal such as a telephone for domestic use. Various ranges of more complex telephones and other terminals would be the next stage of higher R & D cost, then simple key phone and small PABX systems. At a much more sophisticated level, complex ISDN-based PABX networks embodying office automation systems and intra-corporate data/video networks, require considerable investments in R & D. The exception to this pattern might be a subcontractor or a firm which licences-in product designs from elsewhere. Such firms, however, are usually engaged in short-term production strategies or are in market niches. Unless they develop their own R & D resources they will not play a major role in the industry on a long-term basis.

To begin with the individual product project, there are a number of elements requiring specialist involvement which dictate a minimum size of research team. For example, for a telephone there may be a circuit design, physical design including styling, acoustics design and an awareness of manufacturability and test procedures. Specific components such as integrated circuits or handset capsules can be purchased 'off the shelf' but if there is a requirement for firm-specific custom devices this will add to the development effort. One UK firm estimated that for a telephone the R & D team would need to be at least ten people, partly due to psychological teamworking factors as well as the need for specialists. This would lead to a budget of perhaps £500,000 pa which at 10 per cent of sales would indicate a scale of £5 million turnover.

Clearly however, most firms would wish to supply several models and would perhaps want to carry out some IC design particularly for feature phones. This would then accord better with the observed minimum scale associated with component volumes at around a million units or £10–£20 million turnover. Thus it would be possible for small firms to finance development work from lower levels of volume than the industry-accepted production volume. However, small-scale producers would be vulnerable in rapidly changing product markets due to their limited range and would necessarily be high-cost manufacturers because of the absence of production and procurement economies of scale.

For key systems and PABX, the R & D costs escalate rapidly and the cost of R & D becomes the critical scale determinant. It is common for firms developing these products to commit several hundred R & D staff to systems development. Typical figures for European firms range between 150 and 800 (although there are exceptions outside of both extremes). This scale of effort requires considerable R & D expenditure up to a high level of £50 million, and at 8 per cent to 12 per cent of turnover, turnovers of up to £500 million pa. However, within this broad range of firms and expenditures, there is a variation in the extent of systems offered, the proportion of system components designed and manufactured in-house and the extent to which investment focuses on radical innovation (such as switched video for teleconferencing).

Although the scale of effort within the larger firms seemed to be considerable, there were still concerns over the need to expand R & D departments further. Although collaborative R & D was a common occurrence, certain firms in the UK and Germany were looking to increase R & D staffing and were facing problems in the supply of suitable engineers. In one case this was being overcome by decentralising R & D across a number of sites to gain access to a wider potential labour market. Indeed some firms are organising R & D on an international basis partly for this reason.

One German firm pointed out that it was possible with less than a hundred R & D staff to design a small PABX and gain access to one part of the market, but that this could only be a short-term strategy. Even for small PABXs, the trend is increasingly to offer the features and qualities of larger PABXs. Therefore technical content, especially software, was rising. It was thus increasingly difficult for makers of small PABXs to deal with product upgrading without the knowledge gained from the design of more complex systems and without substantially larger R & D departments. It was expected by several major firms that the smaller niche firms would be forced to retreat and ultimately withdraw from the PABX sector completely.

A note on multiproduct scale economies

Although economies of scale in the general sense were achieved to varying degrees by all the TSE firms, the sources of those economies were closely related to the scope of firms' production. In this multiproduct industry at least, economies of scale appeared to be inextricably bound up with economies of scope. This raises the theoretical and practical question of whether multiproduct firms can pursue economies of scale and scope as if they were independent sources of competitive advantage.

The firms do not have the option of choosing to compete solely through the advantages to be gained from size or those from producing related outputs. Both scale and scope economies must be addressed by firms seeking long-term survival in the TSE industry.

TSE firms achieve some competitive advantages through the interdependence of scale and scope economies. These two aspects of cost saving are not independent, neither are they related as simple cause and effect. Rather, the relationship between the scale and scope – the size and composition – of a multiproduct firm's output varies according to the characteristics of functions or processes within the firm's production system.

Compare, for example, economies achieved through component purchasing and R & D activities. In the first case, *scope allows scale* to be achieved. Where particular components are used in a number of different products, a given required scale of component purchasing may be achieved with lower output of each product than with product-specific components. This was the reason why so many TSE firms were able to secure maximal discounts on component purchases without having to achieve disproportionately large world-market shares for any one product. In the second case – R & D activities – *scale allows scope* to be achieved. Output from the R & D process consists of heterogenous information: 'more' R & D effort allows production of a greater range of different research results, product designs, process innovations and so on. In addition, the larger the scale of a firm's R & D activities the greater are the resources available for generating cost-saving products and process innovations across a range of related products. This was the reason why larger TSE firms were able to secure competitive advantages through R & D into, for example, system architectures for product 'families', generalised product styling, 'design for manufacture', and JIT production methods.

These relationships between economies of scale and scope in multiproduct TSE firms are not automatic. They represent potential sources of competitive advantage through long-term increases in a firm's effectiveness, rather than short-term reductions in production costs. The realisation of those potential advantages by TSE firms was closely related to their ability to respond to changing technological and market conditions. These topics are explored in the next chapter.

5 Economies of Scope – Flexibility and the Benefits of Integration

Flexibility and integration

Throughout the international TSE industry, the ability to respond quickly and effectively to changing technologies and market demands was identified by firms as a key determinant of competitive success. Opinions on how best to respond to such changes varied considerably between firms and between countries. Similarly, firms pursued a variety of corporate strategies to implement those responses; for example, firms differed in their efforts to create or control technological change rather than respond passively to the challenges posed by external technical developments. However, there was unanimous agreement that flexibility is an essential characteristic of successful competitive production activities in the TSE industry. In analytical terms, flexibility is also the key characteristic of economies of scope.

Preliminary to a more detailed discussion, three general observations may be made about flexibility in the TSE industry. The first is that market structure reflects corporate behaviour – in this case, behaviour which is widely influenced by potential benefits from responsiveness to changing technological and economic conditions. The pursuit of flexibility is not, therefore, confined within individual firms, but may result in joint ventures, mergers, alliances and other forms of integration between firms. The second observation is that flexibility is evident at a number of levels of activity within firms, and that it is achieved through a variety of means. Flexibility is just as much a key issue in product design, production engineering and manufacturing activities as it is in the formation of corporate strategies. The third observation is that there are real (and often difficult) trade-offs to be made between short-term profit or sales maximisation and longer-term optimising behaviour, aimed at the firm's survival in a complex and dynamic industry. Responses by firms in the study sample suggest that the time horizons of investment decision-makers, and the incentives available to promote long-term planned behaviour, significantly affect the responsiveness of firms. Ironically, those best placed to respond to short-term market changes were those with the longest planning horizons.

The two main sources of economies of scope are excess capacity and shareable inputs. These are examined in the context of the problems and opportunities created by firms' historical investments, their adoption of new manufacturing techniques, and their commitments to standard designs, components and products. The extent and effects of a variety of technical links within and between TSE firms are then discussed followed by multiproduct marketing, a rapidly developing feature of the TSE industry, which is significantly altering the economics of TSE production. Finally, strategies for multiproduct optimisation are considered; in particular, the degree to which TSE firms seek to collaborate with their competitors, suppliers and customers to achieve economies of scope and flexibility.

Capacity utilisation

Potential economies of scope exist where a firm is currently operating below its 'normal' capacity, on the condition that 'excess' capacity is usable for some other form of production. In the TSE industry, the existence of such excess capacity was not seen as a serious constraint on firms' choice of production activities. Only a very small proportion of capital equipment and systems – for example, some plastic moulding tools and some testing software – were exclusively dedicated to single product lines. However, what constitutes 'normal' or 'excess' capacity is problematic, both for the economic theorist and for production management decision-makers.

Results from the study show remarkable consistency in the TSE firms' utilisation of production capacity. Of the 20 firms in the study sample, 19 were able to provide information on capacity utilisation. All but one of these firms regarded 'normal' or optimal operating levels to be 80–90 per cent of the designed capacity of their manufacturing plant. The remaining capacity was either preserved to service peaks in demand for products, or discounted in order to prolong the life of equipment. The one exception, a French firm, reported operating continually at 100 per cent of designed capacity, and servicing demand peaks by subcontracting production out to other firms.

However, this desired-level utilisation was not always maintained. Temporary reductions in product demand, quality-control problems with components, down time for repairs (rather than normal preventative maintenance) and product changes were all reported as reasons for reduced-capacity utilisation. These factors varied in duration and predictability, and in their effects on manufacturing which ranged from slight reductions in assembly rates through to total shutdown of production. These results clearly show the necessity of measuring capacity utilisation over time as a dynamic process; static measures of capacity utilisation are essentially meaningless.

Long-term changes in process technology highlight a significant capacity problem reported by certain TSE firms in the UK and the USA. In each case, these firms were using modern production techniques and equipment, housed in factory buildings that were constructed 20 to 30 years ago. Despite subsequent modification, those buildings were of the wrong size and configuration for present requirements. For example, at one large plant in the USA, manufacturing facilities had been reorganised to completely JIT-based production. With greatly reduced inventories and more compact machinery, substantial areas of the factory building were left empty. Despite running production at record levels, the firm had reduced its space requirements. Yet it was forced to continue using an inappropriate stock of fixed capital. With process technologies developing faster than the depreciation of fixed capital, assessment of production capacity of a firm must take account of the burden of history in the form of unwanted or outdated plant and equipment. Many European firms have been rationalising plants and selling off (or demolishing) factory space despite increased output.

While it is possible to assess broadly the utilisation of manufacturing plant and equipment, other aspects of firms' productive capacity are less easy to measure. Macro-level activities within the firm such as R & D, marketing, sales, management and maintenance all present significant problems in this regard. For example, it was reported by production managers in several firms running JIT-based manufacturing that the best indicator of a plant running at normal or full capacity was the sight of maintenance engineers casually reading their newspapers! The cost of keeping such staff on standby is less than the costs of down time on the line and bringing in external engineers.

There are two reasons why non-manufacturing capacity is difficult to measure. The first is that some activities – such as management and production planning – are not exclusively dedicated to current output but relate to a variety of tasks, including the firm's future operations. Like the car driver who watches the road rather than the steering wheel, management necessarily must look beyond the day-to-day operations of manufacturing plant.

The second reason is many non-manufacturing activities concern the production and use of *information* of various sorts. For example R & D departments produce product designs and process methods, software for products and process control, while planners use the output of management information systems to make decisions. As Machlup (1962, 1980, 1982) and others have pointed out, information output cannot be measured independently of its inputs. That is, the economic value of information output – say a set of production statistics or a new design for a telephone – cannot be assessed directly except in terms of the inputs (staff years of effort, capital consumed and so on) used to create it. Thus, while there may appear to be excess capacity in non-manufacturing activities (for example, due to high overheads) the value of those activities to the competitiveness of the firm may be out of all proportion to their cost, even though they are only indirectly measurable.

Shareable inputs in TSE production

Standardised inputs

The use of standardised inputs by multiproduct firms illustrates the connection between economies of scale and scope in production. In broad terms, multiproduct firms can gain economies of scale – notably through purchasing discounts, better quality control and reduced administration costs – by using standardised inputs at various stages in the manufacture of a range of products. The greater the number and quantity of products which require standard inputs, and the greater the proportion of total inputs for each product that can be supplied in a standardised form, the greater will be the firm's potential for gaining economies of scale. However, in practice, the issue of standardisation in the TSE industry is somewhat more complex.

Firms in the study sample were observed to use standardised inputs of four main types, where each type corresponded to one or more stages in the production process. These were:

1 product and process designs;
2 components and raw materials;
3 sub-assemblies and manufactured parts; and
4 high-level assemblies.

1 Product and process designs
Standardised product and process designs are essentially shareable outputs from R & D which are implemented through product development and production engineering activities. All firms in the study sample reported some degree of design standardisation, although the extent of standardisation varied considerably. In some cases, product designers simply adhered to given technical standards (for example, statutory requirements for suppression of electrical interference) by using previously developed techniques. In other cases, more coherent and deliberate design strategies were employed. For example, one German manufacturer used a modular design for a range of telephone and key system products, such that both the outward appearance and internal circuitry of the products were as similar as possible. Not only did this make effective use of R & D resources by sharing design costs between products, it also allowed for lower manufacturing costs through shareable inputs and gave a distinctive product image for its office-systems marketing effort.

Process design standardisation was reported by the majority of firms in the study sample as a key factor in achieving flexibility in multiproduct operations. Two aspects of process standardisation were observed in UK and US manufacturing plants, and reported by firms in Japan and Europe. The first was the use of a standard sequence of operations in the manufacture of broadly similar products. For example, the sequencing of automated insertion of components, the use of SMT equipment, manual component insertion, soldering, and testing of circuit boards was the same for those used in a variety of analogue telephones, key systems and digital terminal products. The second aspect of process standardisation concerned the relationship between product and process design. A common practice in TSE manufacturing was the use of standard-width circuit boards (irrespective of their length). This allowed the same equipment to be used for the construction and assembly of circuitry for a number of different TSE products.

2 Components and raw materials
All firms in the study sample reported some use of standardised components and raw materials, although firms' definitions of standard components varied considerably. There was little disagreement about the cost-effectiveness of using single types of simple raw materials such as powdered plastics (for injection mouldings), sheet metals, PCB laminates, solder, resins, and so on. Similarly, discrete electronic components such as resistors, capacitors and diodes were seen as general-purpose items and thus subject to the potential benefits of mass purchasing and quality assurance. However, more complex components – notably ICs – were more problematic.

A great number of different ICs are used in TSE products: analogue and digital devices are used to perform a huge range of functions from simple switching and amplification through to signal processing and computing functions such as digital processing, data storage, display control, and interfacing. In addition, higher-level functions that are specific to one or more products can often be performed by specially designed ASIC devices. The problem faced by product designers – and economic analysts – is to what extent these variously complex components can be considered as standardised.

3 Sub-assemblies and manufactured parts
Standardised sub-assemblies and manufactured parts were found to be used across product ranges by all firms in the study sample. Common examples included transmitter/receiver capsules for telephone and key-system handsets and cabinets, racking and power supplies for large PABX products. In addition, a number of firms used the same circuit boards for different products. This had several dimensions. Firstly, most firms made use of standard-sized PCBs even if differently configured. Secondly boards with certain functions were used in several different PABX products. Finally one European multinational firm, in its small switching products, used a standard circuit board and merely populated the line circuits that were required by the customer. Thus two key systems with differing numbers of extensions would have identical circuit boards with the smaller system simply underusing the potential of the board. Savings were possible in the production of just one rather than a range of PCBs and in the single-sized casing.

4 High-level assemblies

The increasing importance of software in TSE products is reflected in the use of the same high-level assemblies of hardware in different products. In this sense, two or more different products may contain essentially the same physical components, yet be functionally different due to differences in software. The clearest example from the study firms came from a German manufacturer. Taking the view that digital switching is really an application of computing, the firm produced a large PABX based essentially on its minicomputer product. All but the smallest firms felt that software would increasingly become the means of product differentiation, and they saw a trend towards the production of standardised hardware at higher levels of assembly.

Two qualifications to the standardised trend were repeatedly emphasised by multiproduct TSE firms. The first was that non-standard inputs, of types (1) to (4) above, often allowed more technically efficient or functional solutions to design problems. In addition, continuing reductions in the cost of producing ASICs and other customised devices meant the cost advantages of mass-purchased or produced inputs were open to question in some cases. The second qualification concerned flexibility. Over emphasis on standardised designs, component use and so on can mitigate against the firms' ability to respond to changes in markets, due to the size of the firm's commitments to existing inputs. Moreover, standardisation carries the risk of stifling innovation in product design – the very ability that market leaders require.

Flexible manufacturing investments

All firms in the study sample reported some degree of flexibility in their use of capital equipment in manufacturing TSE products. There was general agreement internationally that, in this context at least, increasing flexibility meant being able to manufacture a wider range of products using a greater proportion of a given set of capital equipment. There was also broad agreement that increasing the flexibility of large-scale manufacturing capital investments was a necessary objective for firms operating in competitive segments of the TSE market. (Small niche producers, however, saw fewer benefits in flexible manufacturing investments and thus adopted rather different strategies in competitive market segments, namely product-design differentiation or dedicated facilities.)

Flexible capital investments were of two broad types. The first might be called 'general-purpose capital', to include all those items of capital expenditure required for TSE manufacturing but which were not specific to the TSE industry. Examples of general-purpose capital include factory buildings, office accommodation, computers, canteens and car parks. The second broad type of investments covers 'dedicated capital' items which to a greater or lesser degree were specific to TSE product manufacture, or closely related industrial operations. Examples of this second type include electronics assembly and test equipment.

Firms were found to operate flexible or shareable machines and equipment (dedicated capital) in nine stages in the manufacturing process. (Firms which bought in prefabricated components or sub-assemblies reported the use of similar equipment by their suppliers.) Each type of equipment embodies designed possibilities and restrictions on its flexibility in use. These factors are noted below.

1 PCB fabrication
PCBs of any functional design can be fabricated using the same equipment subject to overall size parameters and the number of layers of connective wiring to be printed on the board.

2 IC fabrication
A huge variety of integrated circuits are used in TSE manufacture, and they are fabricated by a variety of different processes. However, all IC fabrication processes can handle different functional designs, (given the required software) often supplied as sets of masks for etching processes. However, as in the case of PCB production, IC-fabrication is limited to handling chips within restricted ranges of physical size characteristics. (This is one reason why wafer-scale-integration-device technology will prove difficult to adopt on a wide scale.)

3 Metal and plastics fabrication
Metal parts and plastic mouldings for TSE products are fabricated using generic capital equipment of given range and capacity. However, the necessity for moulding blocks and special purpose tool bits to be tailor-made for each product means that the flexible re-use of metal and plastics fabrication equipment generally requires additional marginal investment.

4 Automated-circuit population
Two types of automated-circuit population equipment are in common use in TSE manufacture: automated-insertion (AI) and surface-mount (SMT) machines. Despite their different principles of operation, these two types of equipment share the capability of populating circuit boards of any functional design with their respective types of components, provided they have been set up with the correct component layout software. The usual physical size constraints also apply in each case: either type of machine will only handle circuit boards of certain sizes, and a limited number and range of components.

5 Manual-circuit population

Most TSE products contain components that cannot be handled by standard AI or SMT machines. Components such as power transistors, large capacitors, and transformers are added to circuit boards by hand. Very little dedicated capital is required for this operation, beyond standard bench equipment. Flexibility here is primarily a function of the skill of the assembly worker and the availability of the correct components for the product. At one American firm, assembly workers handled up to four different products – each with seven or eight manual components – at the same time, using the same component-assembly facilities.

6 Soldering and related operations

Apart from physical-size constraints, equipment used for soldering and cleaning circuit boards was not restricted to specific products. However, variations in the heat-resistance of SMT components did lead to differences in the nature of soldering and cleaning operations practised by different firms. (Not all SMT components can be dipped in molten solder in wave-soldering techniques without damage.)

7 Inspection and repair

To the extent that TSE manufacturers used inspection and repair facilities for mainline production, few restrictions were imposed by the equipment employed. In most cases, special inspection and repair facilities were only fully employed in the earliest phases of a product's manufacturing history – largely for debugging purposes.

8 Testing

All firms in the study sample made use of automated test equipment (ATE), although the functionality of the tests carried out and the rate of testing varied considerably between firms and products. However, the flexibility in the case of automated testing is completely dependent on the functionality of the ATE software employed.

9 General assembly and handling

A wide variety of general assembly and handling equipment was used by firms in the study sample. The dedicated capital equipment employed for these functions ranged from simple racks, trolleys and jigs – for handling variously sized PCBs – through to sophisticated robotic devices used for component handling and product assembly. The flexibility in use of these capital investments varied, depending on function or sophistication. For example, racks designed to hold stocks of PCBs of a given size were generally restricted to boards of that size, although the functionality of the boards – as sub-assemblies for different products – was not a constraint. (The use of robotic devices is considered more generally in Chapter 6 below.)

Despite detailed variations between firms, a general trend in the flexibility of manufacturing investments was observed. As the life cycles of TSE products have decreased to become much shorter than the life of process equipment, there has been increasing pressure on manufacturing divisions to use the same capital equipment for operations on a variety of products. With some product life cycles now less than 12 months, this trend towards flexible manufacturing investment appears unavoidable. In many cases, investment in large-scale capital equipment specific to a single product could not be completed before the end of the market life cycle of the product.

Flexible manufacturing investment raises two related accounting problems for firms. The first problem – emphasised by TSE firms in the USA – is that investments in flexible plant and equipment are too expensive to be amortised over conventionally accepted payback periods. Manufacturing investment was reported to suffer under a tyranny of accountants, whereby firms' accounting practices had failed to respond to changes in the production environment. The second problem reported by both Japanese and American firms is that flexible investments need to be amortised over the output of several products. Given that future production requirements are necessarily uncertain, none of the firms in the study sample had found a clear and efficient formula for allocating capital depreciation costs between a set of products. Two American firms reported this problem as making the task of investment planning particularly difficult in the face of short-sighted accounting practices. To accountants within the firms, the only available justifications for large-scale multiproduct investments appear to require an act of faith on the part of the investor – most often the corporate finance division.

Technical links

Technological developments

Technological development was viewed as a key issue in responsiveness to market change and, thus, competitive success. Simply maintaining corporate knowledge of the state of the art in TSE product and process technologies required a significant level of activity; the development of new technologies in-house required an even greater effort. There was broad agreement internationally that firms in the TSE industry have strong incentives both to develop or adopt more cost-effective product and process technologies, and to exploit the advantages of those technologies over as many activities or products as possible. These conditions form the background to technological links between the development of TSE products and components on the one hand and telecommunications network technology on the other.

Four trends in the development of component technologies were widely reported as significant factors in the design and manufacture of TSE products:

- The historical trend towards higher levels of component integration continues unabated, with increased use of LSI and VLSI components. This trend applies to both analogue and digital electronics.
- Whilst the development of analogue electronic technology has continued, the use of digital technology has increased, both absolutely and proportionately. There is also increasing similarity – and overlap – between the set of digital components used in TSE products and those used for computer manufacture. There was broad agreement by firms throughout the industry that digital technology would come to dominate telecommunications within the next decade. There was similar agreement that analogue technology would be retained for specialised applications. However, debates within the industry on the future development of electronics tend to be framed in terms of 'when' rather than 'if' telecommunications switching and terminal equipment becomes predominantly digital.
- The increasing use of digital circuitry has allowed much greater use of software rather than special-purpose hardware for achieving functionality in TSE products. Different but related products may contain essentially the same hardware, yet perform a different range of functions for the user. Software was universally reported as the key issue in technological development and product differentiation.
- Circuit boards are also the subject of influential technological changes. Current developments include multi-layering, the use of SMT components to achieve greater packing densities on given boards, and, most recently, the development of 'flexible card' and related technologies. Flexible-card PCBs were first developed for military applications where space and weight were critical, but they are now being taken up for civil applications – notably, TSE products. Rather than having to solder components on to copper film wiring as in the conventional circuit board, flexible-card PCBs make use of surface mount (SMT) components and new materials to dispense with soldering operations. In principle, this very new connection technology is simplicity itself: the flexible board is a sheet of mylar (a form of plastic) on to which 'wiring' is drawn with an electrically conductive ink. SMT components are then attached to the 'wiring' on the mylar sheet with an electrically conductive adhesive. Needless to say, in practice, flexible-board technology is far from simple, with component alignment and the chemistry of the inks and adhesives as critical issues. However, this technology is expected by many firms to find wide applications in TSE manufacture.

  A related but longer-term development in circuit manufacture is known as 'integrated substrate technology'. Here, the principle is to dispense even with the flexible-card PCB and use similar ink-and-glue techniques to mount components on the interior surface of a product's casing. However, this does involve the non-trivial problem of printing or drawing complex circuit 'wiring' on to concave surfaces. An additional problem may be greater susceptibility to physical change. Unlike present modes of manufacture, such integrated substrate products (notably telephones) would be potentially disabled by cracks in the external casing as a consequence of rough usage.

The significance of these technical developments is that they contribute to the simplification of TSE product manufacture. They each affect the overall cost structure of TSE production, although their implications for costs and product design vary considerably. For example, component integration and ink-and-glue board technologies result in physically simpler circuit assemblies and thus simpler sequences of manufacturing operations.

However, the cost of these operations depends partly on the cost of capital equipment, which at least in the case of SMT component mounting machines may be higher than that of previous vintages of manufacturing technology. Again, for example, digital technology – with its dependence on software for functionality – offers TSE-product designers the opportunity to gain flexibility by using the same general-purpose hardware sub-assemblies in a variety of products. This would lengthen the life cycle of hardware designs, while allowing product life cycles to shorten in response to changing market conditions. Here, of course, the critical factor is the cost of producing (via R & D activities) new software for each new product. Software costs now account for over half of total R & D expenditure by TSE producers.

All firms in the study sample identified developments in telecommunication network technology as key issues in the design and manufacture of TSE products. In a general sense, of course, technological links between transmission network and terminal-equipment designs have always been significant. All TSE products can be seen as components of telecommunications systems, in which network and terminal components of the system must be technically compatible. However, the development of digital telecommunications allows radical changes to be made in the functions and design of TSE products.

Integrated services digital networks (ISDN) are the product of the increasing convergence of computer and communications technologies, in which all forms of communications traffic – voice, data, video and so on – are processed and carried as digital signals. Rather than attempting to make use of existing telephony systems, video-telephones, mobile communications, group IV fax machines, and a variety of computer systems. The development of ISDN as a network technology is thus changing the concept and design of terminal equipment, to the extent that traditional TSE products are being subsumed within a much wider set of information-processing and communication devices.

Information flows

Given that the convergence between TSE and computing technology, as well as increased component integration, have led to a need for firms to draw upon a wider range of technologies, how has this been achieved in practice?

Typically, firms split R & D into two types: basic/applied research on underlying technical principles, and development-orientated work on new systems and products. However, a number of different structures are used depending on the organisational structure of the firm's business divisions, and on corporate philosophy towards R & D. Firms recognised that all R & D relevant to TSE could not be undertaken within the product division, as the breadth of technology required was too great. Inputs into TSE were expected from centralised basic research, other divisions and, even in the largest integrated firms, from external sources.

In European and American firms the TSE-based division, sometimes involving some computing products, was the main level for R & D – chiefly product development with some applied research on systems development. Technical links between these TSE research groups and other telecommunications, computing or component research groups within the firm varied in intensity according to historical factors – such as whether they had previously been part of the same division – and to the appropriateness of the work in non-TSE divisions. The most common links were those established with the central research facility, undertaking basic research on materials, components, systems and software.

Central research facilities usually exist within diversified firms for three reasons. Firstly, they carry out research which is not specific to individual divisions, but which may have wide applications. Thus for example, super-conductivity research requires high expenditures and a basic scientific mode of operation. Its applications will include microelectronic devices and circuits, large-scale magnetic equipment, electrical and mechanical power applications and refrigeration equipment (OECD, 1988). Such work is carried out within the central research unit of the larger integrated firms. Funding for this basic research usually comes from a central budget which may include a fixed subvention from each division.

In return for this research fee, the second function of the central research facility is usually to keep divisions informed of technical advances that may have an impact on their specific product area. This includes both internally generated knowledge and external information inputs. Central research usually acts as a clearing system for information from all divisions. One UK firm specifically referred to the role of central research staff in advising the TSE divisions as to which R & D groups in other divisions might be undertaking work relevant to TSE projects. The implication of this, however, was that economies of scope in R & D between divisions of integrated firms were often reduced because of organisational remoteness.

The third role of central R & D was as a contract research unit, assisting the TSE division at certain times with research problems of a more fundamental character than their normal capabilities. Usually in these situations, TSE divisions paid for services rendered almost on a commercial basis, except with the knowledge that information generated within that contract would be available to other divisions in the group, and vice versa in the case of contracts from other divisions.

The Japanese, and some European, firms differed slightly from this organisational form in that there was a greater degree of concentration of

R & D activity within broad groups of divisions. In this way various communications and computer technologies were integrated either within single laboratories or R & D networks. One German firm for example had its telecommunication R & D organised into small groups within a general company-wide IT research network. Different aspects of telecommunications research were concentrated in groups at particular sites, but these bore no relation to a manufacturing or marketing divisional structure. The danger of such centralisation lies in the interface with manufacturing which may be much less direct than in the case of integrated R & D–manufacturing business units. One Japanese firm described the process of moving personnel between R & D and manufacturing as essential to the success of this transfer process.

The TSE R & D unit, whatever its form of organisation, was typically involved in some form of joint research with other organisations, including other firms, universities, public research facilities and PTT laboratories. The nature of these relationships has been described in Chapter 3, but frequently such interorganisational links were stronger and more closely related to product development than intra-organisational links.

Although firms with specific TSE divisional development groups, separate from other telecommunications activities, saw the benefit of focused activity, there were also disadvantages. One firm, with TSE switching products and terminals being produced within two divisions – one telecommunications-based, the other IT-based – reported little collaboration. The two divisions had differing priorities and philosophies towards TSE; the telecommunications division being 'box'-orientated, and the IT division viewing TSE as part of an office-automation system.

The areas of electronics/IT with which TSE R & D was likely to be linked in some way were predominantly components, public telecommunications switching and computer networking. In technological terms these links were largely within component design and software. Even in the case of links between PABX and central office switching divisions, the nature of the technology shared was concerned with components and software used in switching, rather than shared sub-assemblies, PCBs or manufacturing information.

There were rarely close links with capital goods divisions such as military electronics or with electronic consumer products. One major European firm with both telecommunications and military divisions described the main flow of technology as being from civil to military applications. The specifically military technologies were of limited application elsewhere, although encryption technology may be appropriate to some civil applications. The one example quoted of military-telecommunication technology transfer was a military-base-station transmitter adapted for cellular telephony.

Multiproduct marketing by TSE firms

While every firm in the study sample reported engaging in multiproduct marketing of TSE products, their marketing strategies differed considerably. The issue under investigation was the extent to which TSE firms achieved cost economies or other competitive advantage by jointly marketing a variety of TSE products. Two types of strategy emerged, which may be termed 'narrow' and 'broad' respectively. The adoption of narrow or broad marketing strategies depended on both the scope of the firm (in terms of its product range) and its objectives in long-term market performance.

Narrow multiproduct marketing refers to the joint development and promotion of closely related TSE products. For example, more than half the firms which produced both telephones and key systems applied coherent design principles across these product ranges, leading to products of indentifiably similar appearance and compatible functionality. Similarly, producers of digital PABXs and phone terminals typically sought to present those products together as compatible components for communication systems. (Perhaps the most notable exception to this approach was the subcontracted production of standard designs of telephones.)

As all firms in the sample produced a variety of TSE products, so they all engaged in narrow multiproduct marketing activities. The question of single-product marketing simply did not arise; all the firms rejected the hypothetical notion of a viable atomised marketing strategy for any set of TSE products. Given this universal view, it was not relevant therefore to estimate the cost savings or additional sales revenue attributable to narrow multiproduct marketing, compared with individual single-product strategies.

Broad multiproduct marketing refers to the joint development and promotion of a range of products, where TSE products form only a sub-set of those being offered. For example, TSE products are jointly marketed with central office (public) switching equipment, office equipment, computers, and commodity electronic products. Even where firms in the sample produced such a range of products, they did not necessarily pursue a broad marketing strategy. Examples were found of firms maintaining distinctions between TSE and other products – most surprisingly between digital telecommunication products and digital computer/information technology products. However, such historically based distinctions applied in only a minority of firms, in which they were frequently reported as obstacles to competitiveness.

The strongest and most explicit commitment to broad multiproduct marketing was found in the Japanese firms in the sample. These firms actively marketed TSE products as part (a small part) of the convergence of computer and communication technologies (C & C). This technological convergence was described and promoted in various guises by different Japanese firms, yet a common view of its nature and importance was shared by them all. Firstly, the firms all considered information-processing systems and communication products – including TSE – as parts of the same emergent generic technology. Secondly, technical and commercial incompatibilities between those parts – for example voice and data communications – were seen as obstacles to competitive success; these obstacles were to be overcome by technological development and directed broad multiproduct marketing strategies. Thirdly, the direction of technological change towards convergence between information processing and communication was not taken as exogenous. Each of the major Japanese firms in the sample saw themselves as 'technology makers' not 'technology takers'. Each one explicitly and publicly pursued the development of integrated technology for the 'information society' as an overriding corporate objective.

Although the benefits of either narrow or broad multiproduct marketing strategies could not be quantified in this study, available evidence strongly suggests that economies of scope exist in both cases. All firms in the study sample made multiple use of marketing information, produced in-house as a costly activity, or otherwise acquired. Similarly, all used the same distribution channels, sales networks and agents for a variety of products, both for the promotion of those products and for the collection of market and other information. (Some overlap in the use of these facilities did *not* mean of course that all firms always used identical marketing, distribution and sales resources for all TSE products.)

However, cost-saving economies of scope in TSE marketing appeared to be less significant than the benefits to be gained from a high market profile. All the major TSE firms in the study sample portrayed themselves as competent and reliable producers of 'high-technology' products, where technical capability was a prominent element in the firm's reputation. For example, consider the market for medium-sized key systems (found to be an area of strong growth during the study). A firm which already produced a range of key systems and PABXs would clearly have the technical capability to produce a new medium-sized key-system product. By contrast, a subcontract specialist producer of telephones may not be perceived by customers – either individual or corporate – as an equally credible supplier of new key-system products. If this hypothesis holds true in any particular case, economies of scope would exist by virtue of the multiproduct firm's reputation in sets of conservative markets.

These economies of scope might better be described as 'benefits of credibility'. Key issues would include product quality, the perceived reliability of the firm, its ability to make contact in related markets, and so on. A common marketing strategy by Japanese firms, for example, involved selling TSE products to its customer base in computer markets, and selling computer systems to its TSE product customers, as well as new customers for both types of product. Such a strategy would not be open to the specialist TSE firm, even if it had the technical capability to produce an equivalent range of computer and communication products. The competitive performance of firms in the TSE industry may depend as much on their perceived quality as firms, as on the perceived quality of their products.

Flexibility and production networks

Firms throughout the international TSE industry reported facing the same general problem: how to remain responsive to changing market conditions and technological opportunities without sacrificing the benefits of large-scale production. While the firms in the study sample varied considerably in the range of their activities and in the degree of power they enjoyed in different product markets, each firm saw the economies of flexible production as a key issue in the formation and execution of corporate strategy.

TSE firms were found to pursue two types of corporate strategy in their search for flexibility. The first involved the formation of external alliances such as joint ventures, technical linkages, subcontracting and product factoring. The alternative strategy involved subsuming as many TSE production activities as possible within the firm itself. The difference between the two approaches is a matter of degree; external alliances and attempts to implement economies of scope are not mutually exclusive. However, the differences in the magnitude of operations – and range of activities – between the smallest and largest firms in the sample suggest that variations in their corporate strategies are related to variations in competitive success.

The two types of strategy for flexibility are illustrated in Figure 5.1. The simple network models, A and B, describe equivalent technical and market situations; the firms produce three products (a, b, and c) each of which requires different specialised activities or operations in the course of its production. These production activities are shown as nodes 1–5 in each model.

Model A shows a TSE firm pursuing a strategy of variable external alliances; appropriate alliances are formed as required for each product. So, for example, different alliances are effected for product a (1 and 2) and for product b (3 and 5). In this simple representation, the production activities 1–5 are each undertaken by specialised firms. Examples from the study sample included plastic-moulding operations, galvanising of fabricated steel parts, design and fabrication of electronic components, and even subcontracted manufacture of complete products. An important feature of model A is that the TSE firm retains control over the production – including all entrepreneurial and managerial aspects – of products a, b and c.

Model B shows a different TSE firm pursuing a strategy of corporate integration. In this case, the same production activities 1–5 are undertaken in-house by departments or divisions within the firm. Again, the production-control function is retained by the firm, this time by a production-control, managerial or planning department which coordinates the involvement of

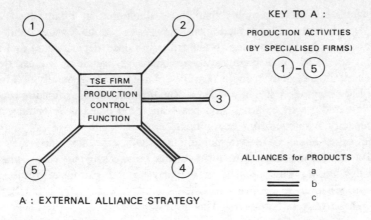

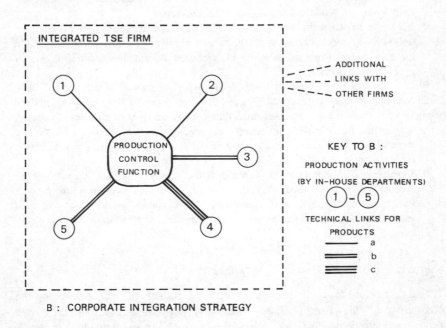

Figure 5.1 Network models of two corporate strategies for flexibility

other specialised departments in the development and manufacture of products. The corporate integration model does not, of course, preclude external alliances; these are indicted as 'additional links with other firms' in the diagram. However, in the hypothetical example of products a, b and c, such external links would not be required except through normal trading relations – for example, in the purchase of raw materials on the open market.

In practice, the flexibility strategies pursued by firms in the study sample were considerably more complex than those illustrated in Figure 5.1. The numbers of products and production activities were much greater, and the links between activities suppliers (other firms/in-house departments) and the production controller were qualitatively diverse. Nevertheless, a clear trend was observed in the study sample. Larger (global) firms generally followed the corporate integration strategy whereas smaller (niche) firms made proportionately greater use of external alliances both for product development and normal-capacity manufacturing operations.

All the firms engaged in external alliances of some sort, and they all indicated a general willingness to form further alliances if and when suitable opportunities arose. This applied particularly to the European firms. As discussed in Chapter 3, the firms reported seeking alliances for a number of reasons. These may be summarised as follows:

- Multiple sourcing by risk-averse firms – which includes component sourcing and some types of product factoring and subcontracting.
- Access to expertise in technologies – TSE products embody a wide variety of technologies; too many areas of specialised knowledge are required for all but the very largest firms, even where the technical information required is strictly in the public domain.
- Cost savings obtainable from specialist suppliers – notably suppliers of basic components and raw materials. Few TSE firms have the capability to produce all their own components, and none relies solely on its own supplies. Similarly, none of the firms in the study sample engaged in direct production of basic raw materials for TSE manufacture; no TSE firm bothered to produce raw plastic powders or steel plate.
- Short-term flexibility – which would enable a firm to change its output level or product portfolio without having to reorganise its investment in product manufacturing. Again, joint marketing agreements, product factoring and subcontracting were common means of achieving short-term flexibility objectives.

Shared use of sales and support networks

Whilst at a broad level firms engaged in multiproduct marketing – selling the credibility of the firm – their sales and support activities were often fragmented along product lines. In some cases this was an inevitable consequence of market segregation, for example between business, domestic and PTT customers. However, in the business market particularly there is a possibility of integration in the *selling* of communications and computer products.

The absence of integrated 'C & C' sales networks arises from two main factors. Firstly, there has often been considerable internal separation of such activities within the firm from R & D and production through to sales and support. Attempts at integration are being led by technical convergence primarily, and consequently sales integration is a lesser priority. Secondly, within the client base, data-processing management and telecommunications management have usually been separate functions, often with differing product sources. This has provided little incentive for integration.

However, convergence does eventually lead to integrated sales networks even if they take some time to develop. Currently, this is more likely in those firms for which telecommunications products are regarded as special-purpose computing equipment. Thus, sales of PABX equipment may be a logical outcome of an installed base of computer equipment. As computer networks spread throughout the activities of the client firm, the PABX performs an essential integrating function and is therefore a key element of a turnkey or system-solution contract.

Other TSE firms with a strong presence in both computing and communications may see the need for integration but find it difficult to achieve in practice. Consequently, staff may come together on a project basis but remain organisationally separate. One large European company explained how they were attempting to overcome these problems by merging the two methods starting with a small number of regional offices as trial sites. Thus, it was hoped to improve sales of both product ranges by targeting existing customers, and trying to broaden the range of equipment sold to each customer.

6 Competitive Manufacturing

Aspects of manufacturing

The competitive significance of manufacturing operations within TSE production varied with the range of firms' activities and with the degree of competition in individual product markets. While all firms acknowledged the necessity of efficient manufacturing as a condition for competitive success, there was less agreement about the most appropriate means of achieving such efficiency. Similarly, a range of opinions was expressed about what constituted 'efficient manufacturing' given conditions of rapid and continuing change in product and process technologies. There was, however, broad agreement internationally that the efficient manufacture of TSE products was inseparable from R & D activities and marketing operations.

In this chapter, the nature of competitive manufacturing is examined in the light of case-study results from the TSE industry. Four areas of new process technology are discussed, as these new technologies have significant implications for the manufacturing operations of firms both now and in the future. The changing role of labour in the manufacturing process is also considered in the context of rapidly changing product and process technologies. The speed of development of these technologies highlights the importance of design principles – in particular, the concept of 'Design for Manufacture' – which was regarded very positively by firms in the study sample. An outline is provided of the principles and practices of JIT methods in manufacturing, similarly favoured by the TSE firms. Finally, the role of manufacturing in competitive production is considered; particular attention is given to manufacturing as one process out of many in firms' production systems.

Advanced manufacturing technology

The economics of product manufacture in the TSE industry depends to a great extent on the technical characteristics of the process technologies employed. Manufacturing technology for TSE is currently an area of rapid development, with changes occurring across a wide range of available capital equipment. These technical developments affect both quantitative and qualitative changes in the tasks that may be performed. In particular, a number of 'advanced' technologies are now available for TSE product manufacture which go beyond the simple mechanisation of tasks previously performed manually. These new process technologies share the characteristic that they perform some operations that cannot be done manually for essentially technical reasons. Four types of advanced manufacturing technology are discussed briefly below, in the context of their significance for competitive manufacturing operations.

Automation

Firms were observed to employ widely differing levels of automation in manufacturing plant and equipment. Explanations of the rationale for automation were similarly diverse. While the smaller firms in Europe saw an investment strategy of automation as a long-term objective of cost-reduction investment strategy, large firms stressed flexibility and quality control as the primary determinants of their automation policies. However, even large firms in the TSE industry did not have the same view of what constitutes an optimal automation strategy in economic terms.

While individual practices differed in detail – for example, according to the mix of products manufactured at particular plants – three levels of implementation of automation were identified.

Firstly, all TSE firms in the UK, France, Germany, and Sweden (together with one medium-sized firm in the US) operated partially automated plant. Amongst these firms there was broad agreement that partial automation was not an optimal strategy and that it was the outcome of constraints on their investment decisions. These firms took the view that their current level of automation was 'behind' that of their most serious competitors (usually Japanese firms). Improvements on partially automated plant were seen to require increased levels of automation in manufacturing, and such improvements were being actively pursued. Some doubts were expressed by senior management about whether small and medium-sized TSE producers could keep up with developments in automation.

Secondly, a number of very large firms, notably in Japan, adopted total automation strategies. In this context, 'total automation' refers to the systematic automation of as many manufacturing operations or tasks as is currently technically feasible, with the consequent minimisation of labour input into the manufacturing process. The role of labour in totally automated plant was confined to maintenance tasks – including troubleshooting during the course of normal production. However, at the pre-production stage of product development, both production engineering and assembly staff were widely employed. This type of total automation of manufacturing was very expensive to set up, and was only viable for large-scale production of standard TSE products. Telephones, key systems, facsimile machines and modems were seen by major Japanese firms as suitable for totally automated manufacture. Larger PABX and other switching products which were subject to extensive custom engineering required a different mode of production.

The third identifiable form of manufacturing automation might be termed 'post-modern automation'. This strategy had been adopted by one major producer in the USA. The rationale for this strategy was that total (ie 'modern') automation relies almost exclusively on the functionality of machines. It therefore fails to take advantage of the most useful skills of labour. For example, production workers develop skills in the detection of faults in PCB assemblies through visual inspection, an ability that is very difficult to build into automated systems. Having experimented with total automation – including a significant investment in robotics development – the firm decided to revise its attitude to labour and capital in manufacturing. (This revision of attitude involved all employees, not just management, in extensive consultation and training activities.) The use of post-modern automation by this firm relied on a recognition that people and machines have fundamentally different capabilities, and that an optimal automation strategy must therefore take advantage of the differing strengths of labour and capital.

Surface-mount technology

Despite being widely available throughout the electronics industries for more than five years, surface-mount technology (SMT) has yet to be universally adopted by TSE manufacturers. Firms varied considerably in their use of SMT and in their attitudes towards it. There was, however, agreement that a range of factors determine the cost-effectiveness of SMT investments, and that 'onsertion' rather than 'insertion' technology may not yet be the most appropriate process technique. Five main factors were identified as determinants of the use of SMT processes in TSE.

Firstly, although a large number of different electronic components are now available in SMT forms, the range is still limited relative to insert-type components. Most TSE product designs still require components that are only available in forms suitable for manual or automatic insertion. The range of SMT components that can be used for many types of TSE products, the proportion of costs that these components represent, and the particular functional specification of circuit boards for current products may all restrict the viability of investments in SMT equipment.

Secondly, the firms reported variations in the supply and cost of SMT components. The market for both discrete components and integrated circuits is volatile; rapid technological change has precluded market stability for all but a few standard components that are widely used across the electronics sector. More specialised and more advanced components are subject to more rapid technological change. This has meant that mainstream component suppliers have often been unwilling to invest in the large-scale production of specialised SMT items for which the market is, as yet, smaller than for insertion components. The general view of the firms was that component and TSE product manufacturers therefore face a 'Catch 22' situation: TSE firms are reluctant to adopt SMT extensively because the supply and costs of components are unfavourable, and the component suppliers are unwilling to mass produce cheap SMT components because product manufacturers have yet to provide them with a large and stable market. However, one firm suggested another interpretation: that demand for SMT components has been growing much more quickly than supply, thus artificially inflating prices.

Thirdly, SMT affects the design of TSE products and manufacturing processes. Surface mounting allows designers to achieve greater circuit densities and faster board population rates than with inserted components. In addition, SMT opens up the possibility of using new flexible-card and integrated-substrate circuit-board technologies. However, these advantages are only achievable if the use of SMT equipment can be integrated with other manufacturing operations. A number of small and medium-sized firms in the UK and USA reported logistical difficulties in the implementation of SMT as a result of existing commitments to products based on inserted component boards. These firms faced two design problems: the first that redesigning existing products to use SMT was costly, and the second that implementating SMT for either new or redesigned products requires changing the manufacturing process itself. This second difficulty points to a more general problem faced by all firms. Changes in the technology used for one or more products necessarily affect the manufacture of *all* related products. For example, the adoption of SMT for new digital telephone terminals would affect the costs and use of an entire existing circuit-board-assembly facility if that equipment was normally used for all circuit-board production. This is common practice for TSE firms.

The fourth factor determining the adoption of SMT is its high initial capital costs. SMT equipment is expensive, with entry-level machines costing around £1.25 million each. (Unlike the use of most inserted components, SMT is *necessarily* an automated technology. Surface mounting cannot be done by even most dextrous hand; the components are too small and they have to be located too precisely to allow manual assembly.) In order to justify SMT investment costs, TSE firms required a very high volume of circuit-board throughput. There was broad agreement amongst the firms that, for the foreseeable future, SMT would not be viable for small-volume commercial production. Low-volume products could, however, incorporate SMT components only if they were manufactured as part of a multiproduct set, where other products would make up the required volume of circuit-board production.

Finally, SMT has implications for manufacturing costs through changes in process-control and correction procedures. Unlike inserted components, SMT components are normally glued permanently on to circuit boards, cards or substrates. This means that errors in the location or alignment of components can be corrected only with difficulty. As a consequence, quality failures in SMT-based-products manufacturing are generally more costly than those of inserted-component assembly where error or fault correction is easier. SMT components are smaller than their inserted equivalents – indeed many are too small to carry any identification marks. SMT components must therefore be handled under the strictest possible inventory and process-control conditions. Some of the firms which used SMT emphasised the necessity of keeping track of the dozens of different but unidentifiable components being used. (Several production managers commented on the costly consequences of components being mistakenly identified.) These characteristics of SMT components themselves and the method by which they are attached to circuit boards impose stricter process-control requirements on TSE manufacture than usually experienced in the past.

Automated testing

The use of automated test equipment (ATE) is related to the functional complexity of TSE products and the degree of quality assurance achieved during their manufacture. Although ATE technology has been in general use in the TSE industry for more than five years, recent product and process developments have emphasised the significance of testing methods and practices.

Testing is generally undertaken at three stages during the manufacture of TSE products as part of the firm's quality-control strategy. Firstly, components and raw materials are sample tested during 'goods inward inspection' – a practice common to most types of product manufacture. Secondly, electronic sub-assemblies – notably complete circuit boards – are tested to detect construction errors such as misalignment of components, and faulty components. Firms reported a variety of testing practices, ranging from 100 per cent testing to low-rate sampling, at both this second stage and at the third stage of final-product testing. With the exception of high-temperature operational testing of PABX circuit boards, physical performance testing of sub-assemblies and products was normally done by sampling. Functional testing, by contrast, was mostly commonly conducted on 100 per cent circuit boards and low-end and medium-level products. Larger PABX products, however, require more complex testing procedures, usually extending to final-system installation on customers' premises.

Despite differences between firms' practices for testing TSE products, three general reasons for the use of automated test equipment were identified by firms in the study sample.

● Manual testing of electronic sub-assemblies and products is inherently difficult.

In the case of circuit boards, manual testing would be counterproductive as there would be too high a risk of the test engineer damaging the board or its components.

- The manufacture of all but the largest TSE products involves too high a throughput of items to be tested to allow manual procedures to be viable. That is, the scale and rate of production necessitates the use of ATE technology. A similar argument applies to physical testing, where speed of repeated test functions is important. For example, testing the durability of electromechanical parts in a telephone requires the instrument to be subjected to tens of thousands of calls. This is only feasible using automated equipment.

- Except for simple analogue telephones the functional testing required for TSE products is too complex to be undertaken manually. For example, even relatively simple key systems allow large numbers of possible combinations of call routing between terminals. In the case of switching products like PABXs, astronomic numbers of functional conditions may have to be tested. Computer-based automated-techniques testing offers the only feasible method of achieving these requirements. Complex testing of products generates large amounts of information which may be used to improve the testing procedures themselves, and the design and manufacture of new products. Computer-based testing allows such information to be collected, stored and processed accurately and efficiently as an aid to quality assurance in future product design and manufacture.

All firms reported growth in their use of ATE technology – particularly computer-based test equipment. The methods and practices of functional testing of TSE products increasingly reflected the convergence of telecommunications and computer technologies. The firms expected that the continued development of ISDN products would strengthen that trend.

CAD, CAD/CAM and CIM

Computer-based systems are widely used in the international TSE industry for product design, and for a variety of control and coordination functions in manufacturing. With the exception of one small telephone producer in the UK, all the firms in the study reported using computer-aided design (CAD) systems for both circuit design and draughting work and physical design of terminals. These systems included analytical functions for PCB layout and, in some cases, integrated-circuit design, as well as facilities for the production of circuit masks and engineering drawings. All the firms reported a continuing increase in the use of such systems; the precision and complexity of their functions had long since exceeded the maximum feasible levels for unaided manual analysis and design.

All firms made use of some form of computer-aided manufacture (CAM) technology, most commonly in the control programming of automatic insertion and SMT machines, and automated test equipment. All these firms reported increasing use of CAM systems. More significantly, they also reported continuing efforts to integrate design, manufacturing and testing functions through the development of CAD/CAM systems. While some progress had been made – for example in the automatic generation of component 'pick-and-place' software (for AI and SMT machines) and testing procedures from computerised design data – all the firms acknowledged that there was still much room for further cost improvement and technical development. Nevertheless, the implementation of practical and reliable CAD/CAM systems was seen by the TSE firms as a key issue in the development of competitive manufacturing-process technology for the industry.

A longer-term goal, which has yet to be even approached by the TSE firms, is computer-integrated manufacture (CIM). The principle of CIM is the automated coordination and control of the entire manufacturing process from product design through to the packaging and despatching of finished goods. While a number of large TSE firms – notably in Japan – are currently investigating the potential for CIM systems, none of the firms claims yet to have implemented CIM technology for TSE production. The closest approximation to CIM in current use by these firms was the near total automation by Japanese firms for production of facsimile machines and modems. True CIM, however, remained for the future. This new technology was considered by many firms to offer an important arena for competition in the industry towards the end of this century.

Direct labour in manufacturing

All firms experienced continuing reduction in the amount of labour required per unit of manufacturing output. Differing rates of reduction were reported, although the heterogeneity of the firms' outputs precluded valid or reliable quantitative comparisons. Five reasons for labour reduction were given.

- Automation. Automation of tasks and functions in manufacturing is achieved by replacing labour with capital equipment in the production process. The rationale for automation is, of course, that the productivity of labour is seen to increase. Increases in labour productivity were also actively sought by firms through means other than automation – notably various financial inducements for labour, and reorganisation of existing capital equipment.
- Quality control. Improvements in quality-control procedures throughout the manufacturing process had allowed many firms to reduce the amount of labour employed on inspection, repair and curative maintenance. In one plant in the USA, repair facilities for assembled circuit boards were left unstaffed, except for short periods during the introduction of new products. Improved quality control had obviated the previous need for labour to work full time on repairing faults that occurred during component population, soldering and cleaning operations.
- Organisation. A number of firms reported decreased requirements for labour as a result of changes in the organisation of production. Plants operating under JIT principles required fewer staff to deal with inventory and work-in-progress

(WIP) stocks.
- Product technologies. Changes in product technologies have led to increasingly sophisticated products becoming physically less complex, with fewer components overall – many fewer needing to be assembled manually.
- Design for manufacture. Along with reductions in the component count, products have become simpler to assemble through deliberate efforts by firms to 'design for manufacture'. This design principle aims for reductions in both the direct labour time required for product assembly operations and the level of skill and/or dexterity required for manual assembly tasks.

It would be misleading to interpret labour reduction as indicating any simple trend towards 'deskilling' in TSE manufacturing. Although some types of skills are in declining demand, others are seen as increasingly necessary. Firms experienced a variety of changes in the pattern of their demand for different types of skilled labour. A consequence of this was that the majority believed that staff training was assuming greater significance and that retraining existing staff was often more beneficial than recruiting new personnel. Such training and retraining needed to be given to staff at all levels in the firm if the fullest advantages of new product and process technologies were to be realised in practice.

Design-for-manufacture

Like many successful innovations, the principle of 'design-for-manufacture' (DfM) is essentially very simple. While all products are designed to be compatible with the process technology available for their manufacture, with DfM this relationship is subject to planned optimisation. No matter how complex or sophisticated the product, the same principle can be applied to its design with the objective of reducing manufacturing costs. Cost reductions are achieved in most cases through the simplification and reduction of required assembly operations. However, it is more accurate to describe the DfM principle in terms of ensuring that the manufacturing operations required for a product can be performed by the process technology available to the firm, given the constraints on the organisation of production imposed by commitments to multiproduct manufacture. While all new products generate some disruption costs – particularly during initial production runs – these costs can be minimised by appropriate product and process design. The compatibility between product and process technologies entailed by DfM necessarily requires designers and engineers to take account of the characteristics of both aspects of manufacturing technology.

For the firms, DfM had become a key aspect of improvements in the competitiveness of their manufacturing. With shortening product life cycles and the requirement for flexible process technology, maximum compatability between new products and the means available for their manufacture had become an absolute necessity for all firms in the TSE industry. Product designs that did not optimise compatibility with the means of production – designs that would require major changes in the function or capacity of existing production facilities – would simply not be viable. The disruption costs to production in such cases would be too great to be recovered within the product's expected life cycle. Perhaps more importantly, the new investment in plant and equipment necessitated by incompatible product designs could not be accomplished before demand for the new product had dried up. This apparently extreme situation was reported by firms to be a very real possibility. With product life cycles of little more than one year – and as short as six to nine months for some products reported by Japanese firms – TSE manufacturers could not afford the disruption costs imposed by incompatibility of product designs with equipment, in this way. While poor design could result in delays in production – and thus direct costs – incompatible product and process design could result in indirect costs through opportunities for innovation being lost. The principle of DfM was seen as a necessary condition for successful product innovation in the TSE industry.

Practical implementation of DfM required product designers to adhere to appropriate in-house and external design standards. These standards apply to both the content of products (hardware and software) and the methods by which they are to be manufactured. The content of products may be standardised at various levels including components, sub-assemblies and complete assemblies. Standardised manufacturing methods were reported by firms to cover a variety of operations. For example, one Japanese firm had achieved savings in both investment costs and product assembly times by adopting a simple standard method for screw fixings for sub-assemblies. By arranging all screw fixings on the same side of products, the firm only needed to provide handling and assembly equipment on one side of the production line, thus removing the need for duplicating equipment.

A more common example reported by a number of firms, and observed at one American plant, was the use of standard-width circuit boards. New products were designed around the constraint of standard-sized PCBs. This was in order to ensure compatibility with existing production equipment.

One Japanese firm emphasised the distinction to be made between standardised *methods* of design and manufacture and the use of standardised *components* in products. If a firm adopts a particular component as standard, to be used by default in a range of products, the firm's rate of product innovation is constrained by the cost and functionality of that component. In the case of sophisticated electronic components such as ICs, where the rate of technical innovation is high, this type of standardisation is a high-risk strategy. There would be a significant probability of the chosen component being overtaken by new innovations offering technical superiority and/or lower cost. In contrast, standardised methods of design and manufacture allowed the Japanese firm to take full advantage of innovations in component technology while maintaining strict control of investment and manufacturing costs. The firm's view was that potential cost savings from standardised components were often outweighed by the risk – and hence costs – of product innovation being stifled by any insistence on the use of outdated components. Similar views were expressed by other major TSE producers in Japan, the USA and Europe.

Designing products according to the DfM principle requires a detailed knowledge of both product and process technologies. Traditionally, TSE firms have treated these two areas of technical knowledge as distinct specialisms, reflected in different job titles such as 'product designer' and 'production engineer'. Those firms which had adopted the DfM principle reported that while product design and production engineering did involve specialised activities and responsibilities, competitive manufacturing and the maintenance of product quality required active cooperation between the two disciplines.

This cooperation was generated in a variety of ways. Three examples from the USA illustrate the point. One firm operated pairing arrangements ('one-on-one working') between product designers and manufacturing engineers, who worked together on product- and process-development tasks. A second firm operated a system of 'product baby-sitting' whereby product designers took active responsibility for their new products by literally moving from segregated design offices to an open-access office on the factory floor. At a third firm, all members of product-development teams held regular meetings to review progress and to work out joint solutions to design and production problems at the earliest possible opportunity. In this latter case, product-development teams included marketing and sales staff as well as engineers. The interchange of ideas and information between technical and commercial staff was considered by the firm to be particularly beneficial, as it allowed direct feedback of current market requirements to the people who designed and manufactured TSE products.

Just-in-time (JIT) and quality control

Firms were unanimous that current best-practice production organisation in the TSE industry was that based on 'just-in-time' (JIT) methods. Similarly, it was considered internationally that the use of JIT had important implications for the firm's quality control, its production costs, its ability to respond to technological and market changes, and its relationship with other firms – particularly, component suppliers. However, the use of JIT methods and their associated organisational implications differed considerably between TSE firms.

JIT methods of manufacturing are based on the pursuit of six objectives:

- reduction of inventories – particularly stocks of components;
- reduction of work in progress – WIP is the stock of part-finished products 'in the system';
- reduction in 'turnaround time' – products are to be made faster;
- reduction in response time for introduction of new products;
- increase in quality of both products and processes; and
- increase in flexibility of manufacturing capacity.

JIT manufacturing has two general features. The first is that the six objectives above are related, such that the benefits of any one can be realised in practice from the other five. For example, reductions in turnaround time will necessarily result from reduction in inventories and WIP. The second feature is that JIT is a *dynamic* method of organising product manufacture – a method that requires continual change and improvement in each respect of the manufacturing process. Successful implementation of JIT necessitates constant revolutionising of the means of production.

The majority of TSE firms in each country had implemented some type or variant of JIT manufacture. The pursuit of flexibility and quality improvement rather than cost reduction was usually given as the primary reason for adopting JIT. Firms which had not adopted JIT methods all reported attempts to reduce their inventories and particularly work in progress (WIP), and to increase the flexibility of their manufacturing facilities.

Among the larger firms using JIT methods, the pursuit of flexibility in manufacturing meant the greatest emphasis being placed on reductions in response times for the introduction of new products and on improvements in quality (the last two of the six listed objectives). These firms saw reductions in inventories and WIP as necessary preconditions for achieving flexibility, with reductions in turnaround times and increases in productivity as additional but secondary benefits. Three of the largest Japanese firms and one major US producer expressed the view that low-cost manufacturing could be achieved by any number of means, whereas JIT methods were necessary for the achievement of flexibility. Their view was that firms which sought competitive advantage simply through cost reduction – but which could not respond rapidly to changing technological and market conditions – would not survive in the TSE industry.

The organisation of component supplies is a key factor in successful implementation of JIT-based product manufacturing. JIT relies on supplies of quality assured components being available at each stage of product manufacture as and when they are required. This means that component suppliers must assure the quality of their output and hold sufficient stocks of components to meet the demands of product manufacturers. Essentially, JIT-based product manufacturing pushes the costs of defective components, quality control and inventories onto the component supplier.

In practice, full JIT requires the product manufacturer to have very strong links with component suppliers, in order to secure 'zero-defect' supplies of components on demand. None of the TSE firms in any country had achieved this position and a number of them expressed doubts about whether such relations with suppliers were either feasible or desirable. One major Japanese producer considered that full implementation of JIT methods in TSE manufacturing would impose too great a burden on component suppliers.

Manufacturing and production in the TSE industry

Two central questions arise from this case study of the international TSE industry. Firstly: what is the relationship between the manufacturing process and the overall production systems of TSE firms? Secondly: how do the methods and practices implemented in manufacturing and production affect the competitiveness of TSE firms?

All the firms considered that efficiency in manufacturing was a necessary but not sufficient condition for competitiveness in TSE production. Efficient manufacturing was seen as an essential precondition for firms' survival in the industry; yet without competitive advantage to be gained from other production activities it would not allow firms to remain as mainstream producers. At best, such firms might retain a presence in the industry as specialist manufacturing subcontractors, subordinate to mainstream TSE producers.

The diminishing significance of manufacturing activities within firms' production systems is a consequence of the rate and direction of change in product and process technologies. Technological change is reducing the proportion of TSE production activities – and hence competitive actions – that are undertaken as 'manufacturing'. An increasing proportion of production activities is taken up with marketing and sales, and with R & D – the process by which new technologies are developed and implemented by firms. This change in the relationship between manufacturing and production in the TSE industry is a direct consequence of the convergence and integration of telecommunications and computing technologies.

There are two elements to this argument, outlined by all of the Japanese and US firms in the study.

Firstly, the increasing pace of technological change has decreased TSE product life cycles. New product development is now a continual activity for all firms in the industry. In a number of firms, management of this innovation process had led to organisational changes, notably closer links between R & D and manufacturing departments. With proportionately greater effort being required in R & D to generate a constant stream of new products, mainstream TSE firms may be characterised as producers of both products and product designs.

Secondly, the direction of technological change in TSE towards programmable digital products has increased the technical and economic significance of the non-manufactured constituents of TSE products, particularly software. Manufacturing is the activity of physically producing hardware. It does not include either the activity of hardware design or the creation of software, both of which are essentially concerned with the production of information via the R & D process. The significance of the software contents of TSE products is rising, both in terms of value added and of its contribution to the technical functionality of products. Therefore, the economic significance of hardware manufacturing as part of the overall production process must fall.

Firms' policies on subcontracting product manufacture illustrate their attitudes to the various aspects of TSE production. The majority of firms in all countries were prepared to subcontract-out manufacturing operations, provided that the technology embodied in products could be secured. In some cases, this was achieved by interfirm technology agreements. More often it was achieved by restricting subcontract manufacturing to relatively 'low' technology products, such as simple telephones for established markets. Products that embodied more sophisticated technology – particularly in the forms of ASICs, firmware or complex software – were considered vulnerable to 'reverse engineering' (theft of design information). In these cases, product manufacture was undertaken by firms in-house. Their argument was that any cost disadvantage incurred through in-house manufacture was more than compensated for by the firm's protection of its technology or 'intellectual property rights' (IPRs). It was only by retaining absolute control over manufacturing that firms could protect their new products long enough to pay off the R & D costs incurred in their design, and then to make a profit.

Competitive strategies in the TSE industry are strongly influenced (albeit unknowingly in most cases) by the economics of information rather than physical goods production. It is the increasing economic significance of information which provides the crucial link between economies of scale and scope, manufacturing, technological change and competitiveness in the TSE industry.

R & D including software production accounts for an increasing proportion of total costs in TSE firms. Expenditure on R & D is necessary in order to generate new product and process technologies. That expenditure is primarily an investment in new and potentially profitable information. Provided that the firm retains control over ('appropriates') that information, it stands to gain very substantial economies of scale from its use. Design information and software can be used at little or no additional cost for the production of any number of units of a given product. For example, software for an ISDN telephone terminal can be replicated without limit for any number of units of that product. Therefore, TSE firms have a strong incentive to realise economies of scale by writing off R & D costs across the largest possible output of each product.

Firms' R & D activities, however, directly contribute to the very process of technological change that is increasing product variety and decreasing product life cycles. The faster new product designs are generated by R & D, the shorter is the 'window of opportunity' available for firms to recoup

R & D investment costs. If all R & D information production was product-specific, the process of technological change would thus impose an investment payback limit on the maximum economic rate of product innovation. In spite of some product life cycles being as short as six to nine months and many others being less than two years, no evidence was found of TSE firms facing such a limit on innovation.

The firms resolved the scale problem – of paying for necessary product innovation – by realising economies of scope both in R & D and in manufacturing.

Firstly, not all R & D output is product-specific. Information in the form of software and physical designs is frequently shared between products, even where minor amendments and further product-specific innovations are added. This means that some investments in innovation (R & D costs) can be paid back through sales of a variety of products over a period longer than a single product life cycle. Examples of this type of information sharing included modular designs for key systems and system architectures for digital PABX and terminal products.

Secondly, the cost of process innovations and their implementation through capital investment could be paid back by applying the same process technology to the manufacture of a variety of products. Indeed, firms had no choice in this matter, as major process innovations took longer to implement than the life cycles of single products. In this way, firms' adoption of flexible manufacturing capacity was a necessary and unavoidable consequence of technological change not only in process techniques but also in product design.

There is a strong dynamic relationship between technological change, the economics of information, and firms' competitive strategies in the TSE industry. Fuelled by the expansion of deregulated TSE product markets and the development of digital technologies (primarily in the computer industry), the rate of change in TSE product and process technologies has accelerated. Firms have sought competitive advantage by offering ever more varied and sophisticated terminal and switching products.

This strategy resulted in spiralling R & D costs – necessary investments which had to be paid back if the firms were to survive in a competitive market. The economics of information – in this case, R & D output – allowed firms to write off the costs of investments in new technology through a two-pronged strategy. On the one hand, firms had two incentives for rapid product innovation: new products could be used to outmanoeuvre rivals, and they could expand the market for technically similar but economically differentiated products (for example, feature telephones). On the other hand, firms had two incentives – if not imperatives – to adopt flexible manufacturing technology: that process technology provided the only viable means of manufacturing the range of short-life-cycle products required to pay back R & D costs. It also offered the only feasible manufacturing strategy in a market where constant product innovation necessarily created uncertainty yet demanded rapid response to changing product demand.

It is for this reason that those firms in the TSE industry best able to respond competitively to rapid short-term changes in product markets are those that adopt the longest-term strategies for innovation and manufacturing.

Part III Prospects and Implications

---

7 Future Trends – the Evolution of TSE

Telecommunications and information technology

The most significant determinant of the future development of subscriber equipment in the short to medium term will be the continued convergence of telecommunications and computing technologies. By the late 1990s, product technologies and their applications will have developed to the point where it will no longer be meaningful to consider TSE separately from information technology (IT) products. Within ten years, the TSE industry may have disappeared – subsumed by the IT industry as a whole.

This process of industrial change will be driven by a number of related technical and commercial developments which are already evident in the international TSE industry. This chapter describes those trends and considers how they will affect the behaviour, competitiveness and, indeed, survival of firms currently engaged in TSE production.

There is already strong evidence of radical technical and market-led change in TSE products, with growing technical sophistication of product designs and increasing divergence between 'commodity' items (notably telephones) and capital goods (particularly switching equipment). Products are changing in parallel with developments in production technology. Major changes may be expected in the relative importance of R & D and manufacturing tasks within the overall production process, reflecting the growing significance of software, or information components, in TSE products.

The competitive environment for TSE firms will also change in the medium term, due to both internal market behaviour and external factors such as the legislative enactment of the Single European Market in 1992. Developments in the competitive environment will affect the relationship between markets for TSE and other IT products. Similarly, the structure of the industry itself will change as TSE firms adopt new strategies and patterns of behaviour.

Although longer-term factors in the evolution of TSE are less predictable than short-term market changes, a number of significant trends may be identified. Demand for TSE products is not infinite, irrespective of the levels of their technical development. In the medium to long term, a pattern of market saturation is likely to emerge, particularly in Western Europe, with varying rates of saturation in markets for different products. The search for, and development of, new markets is likely to alter the dynamics of global competition between TSE firms. These continuing changes in the geography of competition will be related to broader technical and economic developments, in particular the emergence of the 'information economy' or 'information society'. Such developments are no longer merely the subject of academic theory – they are already on the strategic agenda of major TSE firms.

The convergence of telecommunications and IT is not simply a technical issue; it is the outcome of long-term changes in the role of the processing and communication of information in economic activity. This broad pattern of change has strengthened technical and commercial linkages between the TSE industry, transmission and public switching equipment producers, PTTs, the data-processing industry and major users. Changes in the economic potential of information have provided firms in all branches of the telecommunications and IT industries with incentives for convergent innovation. Developments in digital electronics and computing techniques have enabled TSE firms to realise the cost and quality of benefits of digital communications through new products. Conversely, the IT industry has been faced with growing demands from users for data communication products. Having acquired the capacity to process large quantities of information quickly and cheaply, those IT users need to be able to communicate that information in order to gain commercial value from it. In this way, the convergence of telecommunications and IT is as much a convergence of commercial interest on the part of firms in the two industries as it is a convergence of technologies. The new technology will not completely determine the outcome of future trends in the TSE industry, but it will enable TSE firms and those in the IT industry to exploit their common interest by means of increasingly compatible product and process innovations.

Product trends

The liberalisation of markets for telecommunications equipment and services, together with technological change, has resulted in firms developing an increasing variety of TSE products. In general, products have become simultaneously less expensive and more technically sophisticated, offering users an increasing range of functions. These trends are set to continue for the foreseeable future.

Product innovation by TSE firms is necessarily related to developments in telecommunication network technology. TSE products are the principal means by which users gain access to telecommunications networks; these products form the interface – in the technical sense – between users and transmission systems. In the past, transmission technology imposed significant constraints on the form and function of interface products, particularly those designed for data rather than voice communication. Present and future changes in transmission technology – notably the replacement of analogue transmission systems with digital communication networks – are broadening the range of potentially usable TSE products. In the short to medium term, many new products will be based on established technologies already developed by TSE and IT firms. The development of digital technology in all areas of application has built up the potential for digital product innovations. Essentially, TSE firms have the basic technologies needed for product innovation; all that they now require are digital communication networks that will enable users to benefit from digital TSE products.

Within the next decade, widespread implementation of the integrated services digital network (ISDN) in public and private communication systems will have a profound effect on TSE product innovation. ISDN technology provides a common transmission medium for voice and data traffic, graphic and video-image signals and other types of digital information. Indeed, any type of information that can be represented in digital data can be communicated via ISDNs. Further, all information traffic on ISDNs can be handled and processed through digital computation. ISDN technology renders obsolete previous distinctions between telecommunications and computing, and it allows the development of truly generalised, distributed information systems. The terminal and switching equipment required for such systems will be more diverse and more sophisticated than those for telephony.

Early versions of many of these new products are already available. Others, incorporating more advanced component technologies, are currently under development. For example, Oki Electric of Japan describes a selection of terminal equipment products available for connection to public ISDN and private digital information networks. In addition to digital PABX products, these include:

- multifunction digital telephones;

- mobile terminals;
- advanced mobile communication systems;
- multifunction video-telephone systems;
- mini video-telephone systems;
- G4 facsimile transceivers;
- office computers;
- artificial intelligence machines;
- workstations; and
- personal computers.

(Oki Electric, 1987)

Similar views of the product implications of ISDN are taken by a number of other major Japanese TSE producers. Firms in the USA and Europe appear to be more cautious, being less willing to commit themselves publicly to such radical schemes of product innovation.

While ISDN does offer the opportunity for a quantum jump in the functionality of telecommunications systems, it will clearly not revolutionise the use of the global telecommunications network in the short term. ISDN is a systematic technology, which means that it can only be truly effective if the system in use is of sufficient size. The full benefits of ISDN will only be realised in practice once a 'critical mass' of existing subscribers and networks have access to the new technology. The ISDN 'revolution' in products and services can only occur after a significant proportion of the world's telecommunications network infrastructure is converted to digital transmission. This development is highly likely in the medium to long term; major programmes of such infrastructure conversions are scheduled for completion during the 1990s in Europe, the USA and Japan. In the short to medium term, however, non-ISDN TSE products will still be in demand.

The liberalisation of telecommunications markets has resulted in a number of TSE products becoming consumer commodities. Standard and feature telephones, answering machines, and cordless telephones, for example, are sold through retail outlets. This trend is likely to continue, with firms marketing an increasing range of commodity TSE products particularly towards private domestic consumers rather than corporate customers. Many TSE firms see household consumption as a growth area, both in the quantity of products and in their degree of technical sophistication. Current developments include simple key systems, facsimile machines, and data communications products for household use. Expansion of the market for these products is closely related to the development of markets for 'tele-' services such as teleshopping, telebanking and teleworking, and other on-line information services.

Existing TSE firms in all countries have gained commercial benefits from the emergence of commodity-product markets. However, those firms will face increasing competition from two types of new entrant producers. Firstly, a number of established household-commodity producers in the electronics sector – for example, firms with experience in audio and video products – see TSE commodities as a natural extension to their existing product ranges. These firms have the considerable advantage of being household names in consumer markets and they are likely to make strong efforts to gain a significant share of the market for household TSE products. Secondly, TSE firms in the newly industrialised countries (NICs) such as Korea, Taiwan and Singapore have already started gaining a share of world markets for commodity products. So far, these firms have concentrated on the least expensive products – particularly telephones – although some are now beginning to move into markets for feature telephones, key systems and mobile communication products.

Despite encroachment from these two new types of rival firms, most of the existing TSE firms are likely to continue production of standard telephones and other commodity items for two reasons. The first is that global markets for traditional TSE products are expanding, particularly in Asia, Africa and South America, as countries in these regions expand their public telecommunications facilities. As these markets expand, the multiproduct TSE firms will have an incentive to establish a 'market presence' – often including local production of simple products – in order to gain a competitive advantage in markets for higher-value products. In the medium term, any new market for TSE commodities is likely to open up opportunities for TSE and central-office switching equipment, transmission equipment, computers and other IT products.

The second reason is that each large multiproduct TSE firm will need to maintain an identifiable corporate image, based on its ability to supply customers with a complete range of TSE products and, increasingly, a comprehensive range of IT products. While there are strong technical arguments for producers of digital PABX to design and manufacture their own terminal equipment – for example to ensure compatability of products – the commercial incentive to do so is likely to be even more compelling. As product life cycles shorten, firms will no longer be able to base their reputations on the quality or sales of specific products. Instead, the credibility of each firm as a supplier of telecommunications products, systems and services will depend upon its overall corporate image. This argument is very close to the rationale for a number of large TSE firms, notably in Japan, adopting images based on 'total quality' and the message to potential customers that the firm can meet their needs for telecommunications facilities – whatever those needs may be.

Production-technology trends

All aspects of the production of TSE firms continue to be subject to technological change. The development of new component technologies, manufacturing techniques, and product designs all directly affect the production processes used in the TSE industry. Although in the near future the industry is unlikely to gain access to any 'revolutionary' new production methods, it will continue to face competitive pressures for rapid adoption of improved techniques. The short- to medium-term trend in TSE production methods is for fast incremental innovation rather than discontinuous radical change.

Manufacturing operations will continue to be influenced by four main factors: component technologies, process automation, software and organisational techniques (particularly, JIT methods). It is very likely that the relationships between these factors, already evident in the industry, will become stronger as a result of technological change.

The historical trend towards increasing levels of integration in electronic components appears set to continue. In the short to medium term, the use of VLSI and ASIC components will increase, thus continuing the general trend towards the reduction in numbers of components required for circuits of given complexity. In the medium term, 'ultra-large scale integration' (ULSI) and 'wafer-scale integration' (WSI) components are likely to find applications in TSE products which require large amounts of data storage or processing capacity. Similarly, very high speed (VHSIC) components are likely to be in increasing demand for products which need to process large amounts of data traffic in real time, for example in video-telephones, very high quality facsimile transceivers, and ISDN switching products.

In the medium to long term, the physical limitations of conventional silicon-based semiconductor technologies will lead to a paradigmatic shift in component technology. Likely developments for TSE components include the use of alternative semiconductor materials such as gallium arsenide, and a move towards increased use of opto-electronic and purely optical technologies for switching and transmission products. In addition, recent developments in superconductor technology suggest new possibilities for high-speed, high-capacity components. However, these developments are unlikely to affect mainstream TSE products within the next ten years; even if superconductor components become available during that time, they are most likely to be applied first to specialised and high value communication products.

TSE manufacturing will continue to be affected by increases in the proportion of surface-mount (SMT) components being used in products. Higher circuit-packing densities will become achievable and SMT will allow increases in the rate of throughput in production. Increased use of SMT will be required if flexible-card and integrated-substrate technologies are to become economically viable for TSE products. In the medium to long term, widespread use of SMT components mounted on flexible cards using 'ink-and-glue' connection technology could have a dramatic effect in reducing the manufacturing time required for many TSE products.

Circuit fabrication is just one aspect of TSE manufacturing subject to increasing levels of automation. Plastic and metal component fabrication, product assembly and all aspects of testing are also gradually being automated. For the medium term at least, the debate about what constitutes the optimal level of automation in TSE manufacturing appears set to continue for two reasons. The first is that investment in totally automated plant takes time to implement. Even if such investment could be financed, most TSE firms would not be able to construct and tune totally automated manufacturing facilities in the short term, due to the time required for the necessary production engineering to be undertaken. The second reason is that firms currently using partial or post-modern forms of automation for TSE manufacturing are likely to be able to improve their production facilities by incremental innovation for a number of years yet. Given the uncertainty of future product markets, shortening product life cycles, and the flexibility in production required to meet changing demands for products, firms are unlikely to commit themselves to large-scale total-automation programmes unless they can be sure of maintaining flexibility in their manufacturing capacity.

The shortening of product life cycles, together with the convergence of telecommunications and computing technologies, will also change the relative importance of manufacturing and R & D activities in TSE production. There is a clear trend towards increased R & D requirements for TSE products and the consequent relative decline in manufacturing activities. Shorter product life cycles mean that a firm must design a greater number of new products in any time period in order to remain competitive. This increases the amount of R & D needed to maintain the competitiveness of the firm's product range, even without significant changes in product technology. However, the nature of technological change affecting TSE product design is increasing the proportion of production costs that must be taken up by R & D.

As TSE products become more sophisticated and incorporate greater use of digital technologies, the relative contributions of hardware and software to the value of those products are changing. The contribution of software to value added in TSE products is steadily increasing. Software production is an R & D activity, not part of the manufacturing process. Yet software is just as much a component of a TSE product as hardware items such as integrated circuits, PCBs or plastic mouldings. The increasing value of software components in products will continue to influence the relationship between R & D and manufacturing in TSE production.

In the short to medium term, successful development of new product and process technology will require closer integration of R & D and manufacturing activities within firms. Increased turnover of product designs – the consequence of shorter product life cycles – together with growing incentives for the use of flexible manufacturing technology, is likely to result in 'design-for-manufacture' (DfM) techniques being adopted as standard design practice in the TSE industry. Successful implementation of DfM requires close collaboration between R & D and manufacturing, both in organisational terms and in day-to-day operations. At the same time, the increasing prominence of product design and software development in TSE production will provide stronger incentives for firms to seek productivity improvements in R & D rather than manufacturing activities. This trend would reflect the experience of the IT industry, in which the development costs and final value of software have come to dominate those of computer hardware. Technological convergence suggests that firms might gain useful insights into the future of TSE production by examining the past experience of the IT industry.

By the mid 1990s, efficient and flexible manufacturing capability is likely to become a necessary but quite minor requirement for competitive TSE production. In effect, product manufacturing in hardware terms will no longer present significant problems for those TSE firms that survive. The trend towards solving the 'problem of manufacture' will result from firms' adoption of dynamic forms of production organisation, principally those based on JIT techniques. One long-term advantage of JIT is that it requires innovation in production technology to be a necessary and continuous element of competitive production, rather than seeing process innovations as discontinuous, disruptive and costly. JIT has therefore internalised innovation within the firm's activities. In this way, even radical process innovations can be smoothly adopted by firms which use JIT-based organisation methods. By accepting the need for continuous innovation, and accommodating such change through a stable but dynamic method of organising production, firms will be able to devote more of their efforts towards the development and marketing of successful and competitive TSE products.

The medium-term competitive environment

The future prospects for firms in the TSE industry will be significantly influenced over the next decade by a number of broad market and non-market factors. Together, these factors form the competitive environment in which TSE firms operate. In the past, this competitive environment has been principally constrained by the regulation of telecommunication in all countries. In most cases, this involved monopoly service provision and control over the connection of TSE products to the transmission network by PTTs. Whilst public-sector provision and control functions remain important in the competitive environment, liberalisation has provided a new rationale for public policy on telecommunications services and products.

Activity across the whole telecommunications sector is growing rapidly. For example, the Commission of the European Communities estimates that these activities will account for up to 7 per cent of the gross domestic product (GDP) of the EC by 2000, compared with 2 per cent in 1988 (Commission of the European Communities, 1988). In addition to its direct contribution to GDP, the telecommunications industry is assuming greater significance in strategic socio-economic terms as the provider of a key 'enabling technology' for industrial and commercial development. The technological and commercial convergence of the telecommunications and IT industries will strengthen this trend. As the European Commission points out: 'Via information technology, more than 60 per cent of Community employment will depend, to an important degree, on telecommunications by the year 2000'. (Commission of the European Communities, 1988, p. 6.)

Similar analyses of the strategic significance of telecommunications have been presented by, *inter alia*, Irwin (1987) and Watts (1987).

The development of the competitive environment – for telecommunications as much as other sectors – is a specific objective of public policy in Europe. The implementation of a Community-wide free internal market in 1992 will have significant implications for TSE firms both inside and outside the European Community. Indeed, the development of the new internal market for telecommunications products and services is seen as having a crucial role in changing the broader competitive environment in Europe:

> The future development of a Community-wide open competitive market in telecommunications services and equipment will be one of the major conditions for implementing the Community-wide market for goods and services in 1992 at a whole.
>
> (Commission of the European Communities, 1988, p. 32)

In the medium term, therefore, TSE producers will have a twofold opportunity for exploiting the new European market. Firstly, firms can respond to demand across a more open market for telecommunications and IT products. Secondly, they can market TSE products to corporate users as essential technology for gaining access to new market opportunities for users' products. In effect, TSE products are likely to be marketed as the means for firms in all sectors in the European economy to gain competitive advantage over non-European rivals.

The medium-term competitive environment for TSE firms operating in the European Community will, therefore, depend not only on market conditions for telecommunication products and services but also on the general promotion of competition through national and international public policy. The EC countries will certainly present new opportunities for TSE firms through the unification of internal markets, yet those firms will also face new problems. It is quite possible that the lucrative internal market will be protected from outside competition by regulatory trade barriers and by less formal 'Buy European' policies and attitudes. In that event, which TSE firms would be seen as 'domestic' producers to be favoured by customers in the expanded 'domestic' market? Given the complexity of ownership and production relations between firms in the industry, it is by no means clear which firms could successfully claim to be native to EC countries. The competitive environment for demonstrably non-EC firms may depend as much on customer perceptions of 'foreign' producers – and the degree of economic xenophobia generated by new European market policies – as on the actual extent of their inward investment in production facilities within the Community.

TSE and related markets

The future development of markets for TSE products will be primarily driven by two issues: technological convergence, and the use-value of telecommunication products and services. Over the next ten years, two market trends are very likely to emerge. Firstly, TSE product markets will become integrated with those for a broad range of IT products, most notably in the case of switching equipment and TSE system products. Secondly, the distinction between household consumption and corporate investment demand for TSE products will increase, despite a concurrent trend of household commodity products becoming more sophisticated. These two trends are related: both will depend directly on the use-value of telecommunication and IT to households and corporate consumers. Within a decade, the development of these technologies – driven by competition between TSE and IT firms – is likely to expose the limitation of the household market and prompt corporate consumers to evaluate more thoroughly their investments in telecommunications products.

Predictions of market saturation for TSE and IT products are notoriously difficult to make. For example, telecommunications liberalisation radically altered the pattern of demand for telephone sets. Near saturation of demand for first telephones, particularly in the household market, helped to create demand for additional instruments as well as for answering machines and similar accessories. In the IT sector, demand for personal computers by both household and corporate users was largely unforeseen (Forrester, 1985, Introduction). Similarly, demand for mobile communications, notably cellular telephones, has increased much more rapidly than producers expected. However, these examples do not mean that demand for all new TSE products will necessarily follow the same path of spectacular growth.

All TSE products perform the same general economic function: they allow users (consumers) to gain access to telecommunication services, principally voice or data communication with other users. With few exceptions, these services are costly: they are service commodities that must be purchased. Demand for these commodities is price-elastic and depends on the value of the services to users and the users' ability to pay for them. Thus, demand for TSE products ultimately depends on the willingness of users to pay to gain access to service commodities. In economic terms, 'rational' users will minimise their expenditure on TSE products subject to the constraint of requiring the technical means of consuming the desired set of telecommunications service commodities. The greater the range of technically differentiated services demanded by users, the greater will be the need for different or multifunction TSE products to facilitate that demand.

The economic function of TSE products points to a significant difference between the demand mechanisms in the household and corporate markets for telecommunications products and services. These two different demand mechanisms are likely to prove important factors in the long-term development of markets for TSE and related products.

Household demand for TSE products is limited by disposable income and the willingness of consumers to purchase commodities which may have a very low marginal-use value. Consider, for example, the use-values to a household of its first, second and third telephones where each instrument is connected to the same subscriber line. While demand for basic connection equipment (first telephones) depends on the household's demand for telecommunication services, demand for additional products depends on the household's valuation of convenience and fashion (for example, styling of the feature telephones). As demand for basic equipment becomes satisfied, TSE producers will face the task of marketing non-essential goods to households. In this way, household demand for TSE products will become simply one element within overall demand for non-essential goods and services.

In most countries this represents a major change in the market for household TSE products, from a capital instrument owned by the network operator with leasing arrangements for the household, to a consumer rental market. The rapid price falls in the case of single telephones have had two major impacts. Firstly, outright purchase may be cheaper for the consumer than even one years' rental, although low-cost telephones are often different from PTT telephones. Secondly, compared with other household electronic purchases, telephone equipment is extremely cheap, especially given its high priority in most households. This is likely to stimulate the market for additional telephones. However current service usage is quite low with average domestic charges in the UK being around £100 pa. This indicates that for most households telecommunications at present has limited applications even though these may be regarded as essential. New forms of services and terminals require changes in the use and perception of the telephone.

Corporate demand for TSE products, by contrast, is limited by the use-value – and ultimately by the profitability – of investments in telecommunications facilities. So long as corporate consumers are able to realise some commercial advantage from increased ease of access to the growing range of telecommunication services, they will continue to demand new and more sophisticated TSE products. Indeed, where a firm grows through the achievement of advantage based on its use of telecommunications, its demand for capital TSE products is likely to increase. To the extent that these products prove a sound investment for firms, by providing the investor with sufficient value in use, corporate demand for TSE products will become self-generating.

Technological convergence between TSE and IT products is likely to accentuate the difference between self-limiting demand in the household commodity market and self-generating demand in the corporate capital goods market. Again, the underlying factor is the relationship between the use-value of technological products and the customer's ability to pay for them.

The main purpose of convergence with IT is to increase the functionality of TSE products and to allow their interconnection with the broader systems technology of information processing and communications. In the short to medium term, there will be a strong trend towards the interconnection of voice and data communications – one of the key features of ISDN systems, products and services. As more subscribers gain access to these integrated systems, there is likely to be a significant increase in the provision of services based on information processing (for example, value-added data services, VADS), as well as an increase in data communications traffic. In assessing market trends for TSE products, the question arises: who will demand data communications services – and hence new TSE products – and why will they do so?

In the medium term, demand for IT-based TSE products is likely to be confined to the corporate market, together with a small proportion of the most affluent, well-informed and fashion conscious household subscribers. (As in the case of demand for mobile communication products, these subscribers may be considered as part of the corporate market to the extent that their demand for TSE products will be directly related to their employment.) The reason for this market trend is simple: data communications products offer direct enhancement of corporate users' existing investments in IT systems but they do not offer households significant new opportunities for consumption of competitively priced goods and services. For example, consider the likely pattern of demand for facsimile machines. While corporate users may gain advantages from near instantaneous document image transmission rather than the use of postal services, it seems unlikely that households would be willing to pay for such facilities (product cost, plus transmission service charges). Typical households simply do not 'process' a sufficient volume of documents to make the 'home fax machine' an economic proposition.

Within ten years, household markets for basic TSE products in the industrialised nations are very likely to become saturated. Demand for basic telephone handsets, for example, will be increasingly confined to product replacement and fashion-led purchasing by a minority of subscribers. If household demand for TSE products is to be maintained, TSE producers will need to engineer a substantial change in consumer attitudes to telecommunications and in the proportion of disposable income such consumers are willing to spend on product purchases and service charges. In the long term, TSE technology will develop to offer consumers a very wide range of communications media products and services. If demand for all these new products is to be generated in the household market, household expenditure on telecommunication would have to grow dramatically. At present, such a prospect appears unlikely.

TSE firms and industry structure

Technological developments and changes in the competitive environment are creating conditions for change in the structure of the international TSE industry. The integration of TSE technology with IT and the economics of multiproduct high-technology production will leave TSE firms with little room for compromise. By the mid 1990s, it is very likely that the TSE industry will accommodate only very large 'total technology' firms and small niche producers. Other firms will face a difficult threefold choice: expand to compete with their largest rivals, contract and specialise to compete with their smallest rivals, or withdraw from the industry. Firms which hesitate are liable to find the third option forced upon them by the competitive behaviour of their more forward-looking rivals.

Structural change in the TSE industry is being driven by four major factors: R & D costs, production flexibility, commodification of some products, and technological convergence. These factors are related both technically and economically. In each case, economies of scale and scope underlie the development and production of successful competitive TSE products.

Firstly, the cost of product and process R & D is growing in line with the increasing technical sophistication of all TSE products. Product design already requires substantial investment by firms; a requirement that will continue to grow as the software content of products increases. In addition, firms need to maintain the competitiveness of their manufacturing capability by improving the process technologies and organisational techniques employed in production. Design for manufacture of new products will require continued investment in both incremental and radical process innovations. Over the next decade, TSE firms will face growing incentives to share R & D costs either by forming interfirm technical alliances or by directing R & D investments towards the production of information that can be shared between products. The achievement of economies of scope in R & D will become a necessary condition for the development of product and process innovations.

Secondly, the life cycles of TSE products are decreasing. As a consequence, the incentive for firms to employ flexible rather than product-specific manufacturing technology is increasing. Again, competitive firms need to achieve economies of scope in production through either concurrent or sequential multiproduct manufacturing using the same capital equipment. In addition, shorter product life cycles mean that firms need to gain faster access to larger markets in order to recoup product development costs. To be successful in these conditions, firms must be able to use existing manufacturing facilities for rapid production of new products on a large scale.

Thirdly, a growing number of simple TSE products – particularly telephones – are being produced and sold as household commodities rather than as network capital goods. Incumbent TSE firms will face growing competition from new-entrant producers for the commodity market. While these producers may be new to the TSE market, they have considerable experience of the consumer electronics market. In addition, they have large-scale R & D and manufacturing facilities and established sales and distribution networks. The competitiveness of consumer electronics firms in the TSE market will derive from their ability to achieve economies of scale and scope through multiproduct consumer-commodity development, manufacturing and marketing.

Fourthly, technological convergence between telecommunications and IT will be accompanied by industrial and market convergence between TSE and IT product manufacturers. Existing IT firms will have increasing incentives to enter the TSE market for two reasons. Firstly, TSE and IT products will embody very similar technologies, thus allowing IT firms to achieve economies of scope through common R & D and manufacturing activities. Secondly, TSE products will be used increasingly as components of integrated systems for information processing and communication. As the potential value to users of investments in integrated IT systems rises, so will the strategic value of TSE production. It is quite possible that the value to IT firms of own-brand TSE products when used as system components will soon exceed the open-market value of equivalent stand-alone products.

These four factors will increasingly influence the behaviour and strategy of TSE firms through two general trends in market conditions. Firstly, the rate of change in product markets is increasing; firms will need to become more flexible and responsive to changing demands if they are to continue to retain market shares. Secondly, the costs and complexity of new product development are also increasing; firms will need to devote more resources to changing their product portfolio – for example through increased investment in R & D and capital equipment – if they are to retain the ability to produce competitive products. However, it would be misleading to suggest that all TSE firms are equally subject to external market conditions, or that all firms must adopt similar strategies in order to survive and prosper. The growing significance of economies of scale and scope suggests an altogether more complex relationship between firms, markets and technological change.

Consider, first, the position of the largest TSE producers. By any standards, these multidivisional firms are very large indeed, undertaking a wide range of activities with access to vast technical and economic resources. Although these firms do compete with each other and with smaller rivals in particular markets for specific TSE products, their corporate survival does not depend solely on the competitiveness of any particular product. These firms compete by creating new markets for new products, side-stepping their rivals through the application of R & D on a large scale. Indeed, as the rate of product development increases, these very large TSE firms will have less incentive to compete in existing product markets, and more incentive to reap the benefits of monopoly supply of new products. As soon as other firms enter the new market through product imitation rather than genuine innovation, the large producer has an incentive to move on. It can use superior R & D resources to set rivals even greater obstacles in the form of ever more sophisticated and costly product designs.

Thus, very large firms can use their *scale* of operation to finance growth in the range, or *scope*, of their activities in order to survive as innovative monopolists. In addition, these firms are able to plan for large-scale production of any new product and they have sufficient resources available to set prices low enough to create large-scale demand for new products. This type of scale-based strategy can be self-sustaining and, given sufficient initial investment, means that large-scale firms can achieve 'competitiveness' by creating their own markets. Economically 'rational' firms will clearly avoid having to compete if they have the ability to create opportunities for monopolistic profits.

Now consider the likely fate of medium-sized TSE firms. These firms are not generally large enough to create new markets for radically innovative products, although they can initiate product designs and make improvements to them. These firms are forced to compete with each other and with larger and smaller rivals because they are not big enough to avoid competition through large-scale broad-scope product innovation. It is quite possible that any TSE firm which has to compete in the normal sense will not have sufficient size to remain competitive in the sense of the capacity to survive in a free-market industry.

Smaller TSE firms, however, may survive by adopting a similar competitive strategy to those of the largest firms: survival strategies based on the *avoidance* of free-market competition. So long as small firms do not threaten the monopolistic profits of the largest firms they can survive by cornering market niches through specialisation. Firstly, niche producers can develop technically specialised products for markets that are too small to warrant the attention of very large-scale firms. Here, the technical specialist firm can gain small-scale monopolistic profits through premium pricing. Secondly, niche producers can specialise in a narrow range of production activities – for example, circuit board assembly – and operate as a flexible specialist subcontractor to large TSE firms. In each case, the niche firm's survival will depend on achieving small-scale success.

As soon as these firms start to grow beyond their niche markets – for example by developing new products for potentially large markets – they risk attracting the attention of the large TSE producers. If a large firm perceives the success of a niche firm as a threat, the small competitor is likely to be put out of business, either by a takeover or by being undercut on product pricing.

These trends in competitive strategy have clear implications for the future structure of the TSE industry. At present, the industry accommodates three 'leagues' of firms: very large global firms; medium-scale national and limited international firms; and small-scale niche firms. In the medium to long term, changes in the viability of different forms of competitiveness are very likely to lead to a new industry structure, devoid of medium-scale firms.

8 Conclusions

Technological change is both the principle cause and direct effect of competitive behaviour in the international TSE industry. The ability of firms to generate and adopt new product and process technologies is the most significant determinant of their performance as TSE producers. Technological innovation, competitive behaviour and firms' performance are indissolubly linked.

Although competition is not strictly speaking technologically determined, the modes of competitive confrontation between TSE firms are very strongly influenced by the forms of available product and process technologies. Equally, the development of TSE technologies is not strictly speaking competitively determined. Yet firms' design choices about the forms in which new TSE products and processes are realised in practice are very strongly influenced by prevailing competitive conditions. Technological change and competitiveness must, therefore, be considered together.

The competitiveness of TSE firms depends on economies of scale. Firstly, firms derive advantages from being large-scale producers relative to their rivals in particular competitive confrontations. Relative economies of scale are not, however, restricted to the largest integrated global firms; they apply equally to small niche producers. Niche firms survive because they have some special product or service capability to offer. In the supply of that product or service, the successful niche firm will be large relative to its rivals. In many cases, the firm will have no direct rivals – a 'niche' by definition is a small space – and thus competition within it need not be affected by the scale of other firms.

Secondly, large scale makes TSE firms less vulnerable than their medium-scale rivals to the disruptive effects and hence costs of continued rapid technological change. Absolute economies of scale derive from a firm's ability to command sufficient resources – capital, labour, technological information and knowledge – to meet the competitive challenges of any rival. This does not mean that only the very largest firms will survive in the TSE industry. It does mean, however, that for a firm to remain competitive across the spectrum of TSE production it must maintain some minimum absolute scale of operation. That absolute scale represents the threshold of viability for non-niche firms in the TSE industry.

The competitiveness of TSE firms also depends on economies of scope. Firstly, all TSE producers are multiproduct firms, although the diversity of their outputs varies considerably. The benefits of concurrent manufacture of related products are potentially available to all firms in the industry. The firms which manage to realise those benefits in practice gain competitive advantage. Secondly, all TSE firms operate in an environment of continued process innovation and extraordinarily rapid product innovation. These technological changes result in firms facing dynamic scope economies. Even niche firms with very restricted ranges of concurrent outputs may survive long enough to produce a considerable variety of products over time. Because product life cycles are much shorter than the working life of plant and equipment embodying particular process technologies, the relationship between product and process innovation in TSE means that all TSE firms stand to gain competitive advantage from realising dynamic scope economies in practice.

Manufacturing is a key activity through which TSE firms realise the potential benefits of scale and scope economies. Two attributes of manufacturing are necessary conditions for the achievement and maintenance of competitiveness by TSE firms. The first is efficiency: in order to survive in the TSE industry, firms must manufacture products efficiently, in terms of both production costs and product quality. Firms which fail to achieve efficiency in manufacturing place a heavy burden on the efficiency of their other activities, such as R & D and sales. Faced with this competitive disadvantage, such firms are unlikely to survive in the present dynamic innovative environment.

The second necessary attribute of manufacturing is flexibility. Developments in product and process technologies, which lead to the potential benefits of dynamic scope economies, mean that firms must be able to respond rapidly to changes required in the composition (range) of their manufactured output. Investment in plant and equipment must be made with a view to the certainty of shortening product life cycles and, thus, broadening product ranges over time. Capital investment in manufacturing capacity must be appropriate to a number of products to be developed over a future period. Advances in product technologies mean that manufacturing capacity must be flexible enough to accommodate a range of future product innovations. Inflexible, rigid manufacturing methods (possibly adequate in the past) would mean firms were unable to respond competitively to technological change.

The performance of TSE firms depends on their ability to meet these requirements for competitiveness. The six conditions outlined above do not point to one single solution or formula. Rather, they allow firms to achieve competitiveness in a variety of ways by meeting the following sets of conditions:

- the firm must achieve *relative* OR *absolute* scale economies;
  [AND]
- the firm must achieve *concurrent* OR *dynamic* scope economies;

[AND]
● the firm's manufacturing must be *efficient* AND *flexible*.

It must be emphasised that these conditions are necessary but not sufficient for the achievement of competitiveness, in the sense of the firm outperforming its rivals. Simply being able to compete – being fit enough to take part in competitive confrontations – is not the same as being guaranteed to 'win'. In each competitive situation, firms must also meet a variety of specific challenges to produce and sell sufficient products of the right quality and profitability. Competitiveness is a measure of ability; performance is a measure of activity. Ultimately, the performance of TSE firms depends on management actually transforming potential competitive ability into competitive activity.

Conventional economic theory implies that competition between firms in product markets is a simple process, characterised by stability, or at least predictable change. Empirical investigation of the international TSE industry suggests quite the opposite: that competition is a complex process, which occurs in a rapidly changing technological and commercial environment. The competitiveness of firms in the TSE industry depends to a large extent on their ability to respond to changes in that environment. Competitiveness is therefore a dynamic attribute of firms, which varies over time. It may be won or lost according to the firm's responses to changing technological opportunities and market conditions within a particular industry as its structure changes over time.

At first glance, the international market for TSE products appears to be sufficiently segmented and differentiated to allow some firms to avoid direct competitive confrontation if they choose to do so. Subscriber equipment includes a very wide range of products, which differ considerably in technical sophistication, and which are designed to meet frequently incompatible technical standards. However, firms in the TSE industry do confront one another in a variety of competitive situations. Their performance, relative to each other, in securing competitive advantage determines both individual firms' survival and prosperity and the long-term capacity and structure of the industry. Just how and why do TSE firms compete?

This study suggests that firms in the TSE industry engage in competition at three distinct levels, each one differently influenced by the costs and advantages of technological change. At each level, firms face choices about whether or not to compete, and about what strategies and modes of behaviour to adopt in order to gain advantage over rivals.

Firstly, firms engage in 'product specific competition'. For example, there are a number of competing suppliers for simple non-ISDN telephones approved for connection to the UK public telecommunications network. These products are identifiably different to those supplied for use in other countries and, therefore, the market for them is geographically restricted.

Similarly, markets for other TSE products may be narrowly defined (although in some cases these markets are not restricted by individual national boundaries).

In this type of 'competition', only a small number of TSE firms (typically two or three) were involved in contesting each narrowly defined market. For each market, a small sub-set of firms in the industry chose to compete for the supply of a particular product. Different markets were contested by different groups of firms. For each firm in the industry, therefore, competitiveness in product supply depended both on the firm's ability to produce goods with a high quality:price ratio and on its choice of which particular markets to enter. This type of competition is characterised by short-term decisions and behaviour of firms.

Secondly, firms engage in 'market-group competition'. At this level they compete by maintaining or expanding their presence in groups of related markets. Here, firms are faced with making medium-term commitments to the manufacture of related types of products, irrespective of short-term decisions to produce any specific individual product. For example, a number of TSE firms face a choice of whether to manufacture telephones (of any sort) given the decision of large established consumer electronics firms to enter the 'market group' for telephones as commodity producers.

Market-group competition typically involved substantial numbers of firms for each product type (telephones, key systems, PABX, fax machines and so on). While a large sub-set of TSE firms competed in each market group, there was no product type which involved competition between all TSE firms. Even at this quite broad level of market description, competition in the industry was still qualified by the differing composition of firms' outputs. Therefore, even though 'market group competition' characterised the behaviour of all firms in the industry, this did not mean that all those firms continually competed directly with each other in any group of markets.

Thirdly, all TSE firms engaged in 'strategic competition' either deliberately or reactively. At this level, firms make major decisions about their objectives, activities, and, indeed, their corporate identity and survival. For example, they are faced with choices about whether to continue manufacturing TSE products of any sort; whether to increase their involvement in IT production; whether to produce telecommunications or information services; whether to engage in strategic alliances with other firms; or to pursue corporate takeovers or mergers.

Strategic competition is an altogether different process to product-supply or market-group competition. Activity at the long-term strategic level results in changes in the structure and capacity of the international industry. In this context, competitiveness is more concerned with firms' managerial, innovative and productive potential – notably through economies of scale and scope – than with the short- to medium-term profitability of particular TSE products. Viewed from the broad perspective of established profit-seeking

TSE firms, being competitive must include the ability to enter new (non-TSE) markets and, if necessary, to exit from TSE markets without incurring unacceptable costs.

Competitiveness must be treated as an active concept. At each of the three levels of competition, competitiveness means not only making decisions to confront rival firms in appropriate ways, but also implementing those decisions effectively. If a firm is seen not to act on its potential ability to engage in product-supply, market-group or strategic competitive situations, it will not effectively be capable of challenging or meeting the challenges of other firms. As a dynamic attribute of the firm, competitiveness depends on translating ability into action.

From the study, two conclusions can be drawn. Firstly, successful firms are those that adopt appropriate strategies for different types of competitive situations. They understand that each type of competition involves different rules of engagement and behave accordingly.

Secondly, industrial and regulatory policies which seek to promote the performance of multiproduct firms must take account of the variety of competitive situations facing those firms. Simply encouraging competitiveness in a narrow, ill-defined sense is not enough; firms themselves understand very well that competition in the real world is a complex business. Industrial policy and regulations must reflect the same understanding if they are not to inhibit the international competitive performance of firms in the industry.

Glossary of Terms

analogue (technology)	Speech/data transmission involving modulated wave forms where the characteristics of the wave describe the sound transmitted. Data are transformed into sound signals for transmission (cf digital technology).
ASIC	Application-specific integrated circuits are integrated circuits (see IC) designed for a specific use, either as a fully customised device or as a semi-customised device whereby the ASIC is based on a standard format.
automated test equipment (ATE)	Pre-programmable equipment for testing the integrity of circuits, particularly applied to printed circuit boards in TSE. The circuit is tested by applying a pre-set sequence of voltages at certain points on the board, and automatically comparing results with norms.
basic services	(see also VADS, enhanced services). Telecommunications services provided within the public network that allow subscribers to use the network. Essentially transmission services.
CAD	Computer-aided design.
CAD/CAM	Computer-aided design/computer-aided manufacture.
CCITT	International Telegraph and Telephone Consultative Committee.
cellular telephony	A mobile radio telecommunications system involving the use of small 'cells' containing transmitter–receivers. Radio frequencies can be re-used in distant cells

	to maximise usage of the band width.
central office equipment	(see public switching equipment).
centrex	Centrex services are those supplied by central switching equipment rather than by local private switches (PABX) or telephone/terminal equipment. Centrex services are provided at a cost by the telecommunications carrier (often the PTT).
CIM	Computer-integrated manufacture.
circuit population	The process of placing electronic components into a circuit on a printed circuit board, thus populating the base board with active or passive components. Population includes both insertion and onsertion (surface-mount) techniques.
CPE	Customer-premises equipment (US term); alternative name for TSE.
digital (technology)	Speech/data transmission by means of discrete signals coded to represent the type of information being communicated. All types of information are transmitted as digital data; in principle, all such data can be transformed or processed using digital computation techniques, (cf analogue technology).
enhanced services	(see also basic services, VADS). Tele-communication services provided over a public or private network either by the network operator or another party which enhance, or add value to the network, usually by providing information. Such services are charged at a higher rate by the network operator and revenue is passed on to the service provider.
ESPRIT	European Strategic Programme for Research and Development in Information Technology. A pre-competitive collaborative research programme funded by the European Communities.
fax	Facsimile transmission (terminal, system etc).
flexible-card technology	New type of printed circuit board technology, in which electronic

	components are mounted on thin flexible materials (usually plastics) rather than on rigid boards. Flexible cards allow the use of non-soldered connections between components.
IC	Integrated circuit.
integrated substrate technology	A new method of constructing circuits by mounting electronic components and connections directly on to the structure of a product (eg a telephone casing) rather than on to a separate circuit board.
interactive cable	Broadband cable network used to deliver television services which may additionally be used for information transmission in both directions including – in principle – telecommunications.
internal-line circuits	Circuits within a PABX that switch and control access to internal telephone extensions. Each extension will have a separate line circuit.
ISDN	Integrated Service Digital Network. A new form of public telecommunications network using digital technology to combine voice and data applications. ISDN is a standard form set by the CCITT.
JIT	'Just-in-Time' method of organising manufacture of products: key characteristics are minimal inventories at each stage of production, responsiveness to changes required in output levels or composition, and tight quality control.
key system	A small-scale PABX which may be integrated within a telephone terminal or may be of desk-top scale. This compares with a freestanding racked PABX. Number of extensions usually ranges from two up to 100. The key system does not require a separate operator and calls can be taken from any terminal.
LAN	Local area network: private computer-based communication network that is local to a single site (eg an office block or manufacturing plant).

modem	A modulator/demodulator device to transform digital computer signals to analogue signals for transmission over analogue telecommunication networks.
PABX	Private automatic branch exchange.
PCB	Printed circuit board.
PTT	Postal, telegraph and telecommunications administration.
public switching equipment	The switching mechanisms within the public telecommunications network which connect subscriber lines via trunk lines to each other. The network is comprised of switches connected by transmission lines.
RACE	R & D in advanced communication technologies in Europe.
SIC	Standard Industrial Classification. Classification scheme for sectors and industries, using a nested hierarchy of codes to describe disaggregated industries: extends to five digits in the UK. In other countries, other names may be used.
surface-mount technology (SMT)	Technique of fixing electronic components on to the surface of a printed circuit board or other circuit substrate, rather than inserting pinned components into holes in circuit boards.
telematics	A generic term to describe telecommunications services other than voice telephony.
teletex	A specialised form of data communications between word processors, computers or electronic typewriters. It operates over the public network using a standard eight-bit code for sending messages between office terminals. It is intended to replace telex.
teletext	(see videotex).
TSE	Telecommunications subscriber equipment (see also CPE). Telecommunications equipment installed on subscriber's premises which usually allows the subscriber to gain access to public telecommunications networks.
type approval	Permission from a regulatory body to

supply telecommunications products of a type or model submitted for testing, to be connected to the public network. The product is thus deemed to conform to national standards and will not inflict damage on the network.

VADS — Value-added data services.

VANS — Value-added network services.

videotex — Data services transmitted via telecommunications networks and accessed via adapted video displays. Also known as viewdata (eg 'Prestel' in the UK).

work in progress (WIP) — Stock of part-finished products held within a manufacturing process. WIP generally excludes inventory stocks of unused components and buffer stocks of finished products awaiting distribution.

References

Abernathy, W.J., Clark, K.B. and Kantrow, A.M., 1983: *Industrial renaissance: producing a competitive future for America*, Basic Books, New York.

Alchian, A., 1963: 'Reliability of progress issues in airframe production', *Econometrica*, 31, pp. 679–93.

Ames, E. and Rosenberg, N., 1963: 'Changing technological leadership and industrial growth', *Economic Journal*, March 1963, pp. 13–31.

Atkinson, J. and Meagen, N., 1986: *Changing working patterns: how companies achieve flexibility to meet new needs*, a report by the Institute of Manpower Studies for the National Economic Development Office in association with the Department of Employment, NEDO, London.

Bailey, E.E. and Friedlaender, A.F., 1982: 'Market structure and multiproduct industries', *Journal of Economic Literature*, vol. XX, September 1982, pp. 1024–48.

Bain, J.S., 1959: *Industrial organisation*, John Wiley & Sons, New York.

Baker, V.P., Chambers, W., Taylor, F. and Tester, N.W., 1985: 'Design and manufacture of a new telephone transmitter/review capsule', *Proceedings of the Institution of Mechanical Engineers*, 199, pp. 189–96.

Baloff, N., 1966: 'The learning curve – some controversial issues', *Journal of Industrial Economics*, XIV, 275–82.

Baughcum, A., 1986: 'Deregulation, divestiture and competition in US telecommunications: lessons for other countries', in Snow M.S., ed., *Telecommunications regulation and deregulation in industrialised democracies*, pp. 69–105, North-Holland, Amsterdam.

Baumol, W.J., 1982: 'Contestable markets: an uprising in the theory of industry structure', *American Economic Review* 72, (1), pp. 1–15.

Bain, J.S., 1956: *Barriers to new competition: their character and consequences in manufacturing industries*, Harvard University Press, Cambridge, Mass.

BEQB, 1982: 'Measures of competitiveness', *Bank of England Quarterly Bulletin*, September, pp. 369–75.

Bilas, R.A., 1967: *Microeconomic theory – a graphical analysis*, McGraw-Hill, New York.

Branton, N. and Livingstone, J.M., 1979: *Managerial economics in practice*, Hodder and Stoughton, London.

Business, 1987: January, 'Fax of life', pp. 68–70.

Business Week, 1988: 21 March, 'It's a fax, fax, fax, fax, world', p. 81.

Buzzell, R.D., 1983: 'Is vertical integration profitable?', *Harvard Business Review*, 61, (1), pp. 92–102.

Casson, M., 1987: *The firm and the market: studies in multinational enterprise and the scope of the firm*, MIT Press, Cambridge, Mass.

Commission of the European Communities, 1988: 'Towards a competitive community-wide telecommunication market in 1992: implementing the Green Paper on the development of the common market for telecommunication services and equipment', *COM (88) 48*, CEC, Brussels.

Commission of the European Communities, 1987: 'Towards a dynamic European economy: Green Paper on the development of the Common Market for telecommunication services and equipment', *COM (87) 290*, CEC, Brussels.

De Lamarter, R.T., 1987: *Big Blue: IBM's use and abuse of power*, Macmillan, London.

Dickson, K. and Sciberras, E., 1985: *Technical change and international competitiveness in the food processing equipment industry*, Technical Change Centre, London.

Economist, 17.10.1987, 'New Lines for old: a survey of telecommunications'.

Electronic Industries Association of Japan, 1986: *Facts and figures on the Japanese electronic industry 1986*, EIAJ, Tokyo.

Financial Times, 19.10.1987, World telecommunications supplement.

Forrester, T., 1985: *The information technology revolution*, Basil Blackwell, Oxford.

Freeman, C., 1974: *The economics of industrial innovation*, Penguin, London.

Galbraith, J.K., 1952: *American capitalism*, Houghton-Mifflin, Boston.

Gold, B., 1968: 'New perspectives on cost theory and empirical findings', *Journal of Industrial Economics*, 14, pp. 163–97.

Gold, B., 1981: 'Changing perspectives on size, scale and returns: an interpretive survey', *Journal of Economic Literature*, XIX, pp. 5–33.

Goldhar, J.D. and Jelinek, M., 1983: 'Plan for economies of *scope*', *Harvard Business Review* 61, (6), pp. 141–8.

Guardian, 21.6.1984, London.

Hakansson, H., ed., 1987: *Industrial development: a network approach*, Croom Helm, London.

Hay, D.A. and Morris, D.J., 1979: *Industrial economics: theory and evidence*, Oxford University Press, Oxford.

Hills, J., 1986: *Deregulating telecoms: competition and control in the Unites States, Japan and Britain*, Frances Pinter, London.

Hyer, N.L. and Wemmerlov, U., 1984: 'Group technology and productivity', *Harvard Business Review* 62, (4), pp. 140–9.

Irwin, M.R., 1987: 'The fusion of telecommunications and corporate strategy', in Estabrooks M.F. and Rodolphe, H.L., eds., *Telecommunications: a strategic perspective on regional, economic and business development*, Canadian Institute for Research on Regional Development, Moncton.

Ito, Y., 1986: 'Telecommunications and industrial policies in Japan: recent developments', in Snow M.S., ed., *Telecommunications regulation and deregulation in industrial democracies*, North-Holland, Amsterdam.

Kaplinsky, R., 1984: *Automation – the technology and society*, Longman, Harlow.

Kamien, M.I. and Schwartz, N.L., 1975: 'Market structure and innovation: a survey', *Journal of Economic Literature*, 13, pp. 1–37.

Kobayashi, K., 1986: 'Quality management at NEC corporation', *IEE Communications Magazine*, 24, (5), pp. 5–9.

Law, C.E., 1986: *Cellular communications 1986: a worldwide report*, Mintel/Cellnet, London.

Lipsey, R., 1971: *An introduction to positive economics*, Weidenfeld and Nicolson, London (3rd edn).

Machlup, F., 1962: *The production and distribution of knowledge in the United States*, Princetown University Press, Princeton, N.J.

Machlup, F., 1980: *Knowledge: its creation, distribution and economic significance*, vol. I: *Knowledge and knowledge production*, Princeton University Press, Princeton, N.J.

Machlup, F., 1982: *Knowledge: its creation, distribution and economic significance*, vol. II: *The Branches of Learning*, Princeton University Press, Princeton, N.J.

Mansfield, E., 1980: *Principles of microeconomics*, W.W. Norton and Co., New York (3rd edn).

Massey, D. and Meegan, R.A., 1979: 'The geography of industrial reorganisation: the spatial effects of restructuring of the electrical engineering sector under the industrial reorganisation corporation', *Progress in Planning*, 10, (3), pp. 155–237.

Miller, E.M., 1977a: 'Size of firm and size of plant', *Southern Economic Journal*, 44, pp. 861–72.

Miller, E.M., 1977b: 'The extent of economies of scale: the effects of firm size on labour productivity and usage rates', *Southern Economic Journal*, 44, pp. 470–87.

Miller, J., 1988: 'Telecommunications in the Americas', South Special Report, *South*, 90, pp. 65–7.

Monopolies and Mergers Commission, 1986a: 'British Telecommunications PLC and Mitel Corporation: a report on the proposed merger', *Cmnd 9715*, HMSO, London.

Monopolies and Mergers Commission, 1986b: 'The General Electric Company PLC and The Plessey Company PLC: a report on the proposed merger', *Cmnd 9867*, HMSO, London.

Morgan, K. and Webber, D., 1986: 'Divergent paths: political strategies for telecommunications in Britain, France and West Germany', in K. Dysan and P Humphreys, eds., *The politics of the communications revolution in Western Europe*, Frank Cass, London.

Mueller, D.C. and Tilton, J.E., 1969: 'Research and development costs as a barrier to entry', *Canadian Journal of Economics*, 2, pp. 570–9.

Naegele, T., 1987: 'Staying home: how some US producers fight back', *Electronics* June 25, pp. 80–4.

Narjes, K-H, 1988: 'Towards a European telecommunications community: implementing the Green Paper', *Telecommunications Policy*, 12, pp. 106–8.

OECD, 1983: *Telecommunications: pressures and policies for the change*, Organisation for Economic Cooperation and Development, Paris.

OECD, 1987: *Trends of Change in Telecommunications Policy*, Organisation for Economic Cooperation and Development, Paris.

OECD, 1988: 'The technological and economic impacts of the new superconductors', *OECD STI Review*, 3, pp. 99–134.

Oki Electric, 1987: *Annual Report 1987*, Tokyo: Oki Electric Industry Company Limited, Tokyo.

O'Reilly, W.P., 1986: *Computer-aided electronic engineering*, Van Nostrand Reinhold (UK), Wokingham, Berks.

Panzar, J.C. and Willig, R.D., 1981: 'Economies of scope', *American Economic Review*, vol. 71, no. 2, pp. 268–72.

Peck, F. and Townsend, A., 1984: 'Contrasting experience of recession and spatial restructuring: British shipbuilders, Plessey and Metal Box', *Regional Studies*, 18, pp. 319–38.

Penrose, E., 1959: *The theory of the growth of the firm*, Basil Blackwell, Oxford.

Pettigrew, A., 1985: *The awakening giant: continuity and change in Imperial Chemical Industries*, Basil Blackwell, Oxford.

Policy Studies Institute, 1986: *Factors affecting business competitiveness in Britain: implications and proposals for the design of a research programme*, PSI, London.

Porter, M., 1980: *Competitive strategy: techniques for analysing industries and competitors*, Free Press, New York.

Porter, M., 1983: 'The technological dimension of competitive strategy', *Research on technological innovation, management and policy*, 1, pp. 1–33.

Porter, M.E., 1985: *Competitive advantage: creating and sustaining superior performance*, Free Press, New York.

Pratten, C.F., 1971: *Economies of scale in manufacturing industry*, Occasional Paper no. 28, University of Cambridge Dept. of Applied Economies, CUP, Cambridge.

Radner, R., 1986: 'The internal economy of large firms', *Supplement to the Economic Journal* 96, Conference Papers 1–22.

Richardson, J., 1986: 'Policy, politics and the communications revolution in Sweden', in K. Dysan and P. Humphreys, eds., *The Politics of the Communication Revolution in Western Europe*, Frank Cass, London.

Robinson, E.A.G., 1931: *The structure of competitive industry*, Cambridge University Press, Cambridge.

Rosegger, G., 1980: *The economics of production and innovation: an industrial perspective*, Pergamon Press, Oxford.

Roulet, M., 1988: 'France telecom: preparing for more competition', *Telecommunications Policy*, 12, pp. 109–13.

Sciberras, E. and Payne, B., 1985: *Technical change and international competitiveness 1: machine tool industry*, Longman, Harlow.

Sciberras, E. and Payne, B., 1986: *Technical change and international competitiveness 2: telecommunications industry*, Longman, Harlow.

Sharp, M. and Shearman, C., 1987: 'European technological collaboration', *Chatham House Papers 36*, RIIA/Routledge & Kegan Paul, London.

Shepherd, W.G., 1984: '"Contestability" vs competition', *American Economic Review*, 74, (4), pp. 572–87.

Silberston, A., 1972: 'Economies of scale in theory and practice', *Economic Journal*, 82, pp. 369–91.

Skinner, W., 1974: 'The focused factory', *Harvard Business Review*, May–June, pp. 113–21.

Stobaugh, R. and Telesio, P., 1983: 'Match manufacturing policies and product strategy', *Harvard Business Review* 61, (2), pp. 113–20.

Swann, P., 1986: *Quality innovation: an economic analysis of rapid improvements in microelectronic components*, Frances Pinter, London.

Teli, 1986: *Annual Report*, Teli AB, Stockholm.

Tunstall, J., 1986: *Communications deregulation: the unleashing of the American communications industry*, Basil Blackwell, Oxford.

United Nations Centre on Transnational Corporations, 1986: *Transnational corporations in the international semiconductor industry*, United Nations, New York.

Walton, R.E. and Sussman, G.I., 1987: 'People policies for the new machines', *Harvard Business Review*, March/April, pp. 98–106.

Watts, T., 1983: 'Telecommunications policy, productivity and strategies of multinational corporations in the transition to an information economy' in Estabrooks M.R. and Rodolphe H.L., eds., 1987, *Telecommunications: a strategic perspective on regional, economic and business development*, Canadian Institute for Research on Regional Development, Moncton.

Willats, P., 1982: 'National telecommunications strategies, government interference or framework for competitiveness', *The changing basis of competition in the 80s*, 5th Executive Forum in International Communications, Arthur D. Little, Boston, Mass.

Index